The
Young
Writer's
Handbook

The Young Writer's Handbook

Allan A. Glatthorn / Willa F. Spicer

McDougal, Littell & Company

Evanston, Illinois
New York   Dallas   Sacramento

THE AUTHORS

Allan A. Glatthorn is Associate Professor of English Education, Graduate School of Education, University of Pennsylvania.

Willa F. Spicer is Director of Curriculum and Instruction, South Brunswick (N.J.) Public Schools.

Copyright © 1988 by McDougal, Littell & Company
Box 1667, Evanston, Illinois 60204
All rights reserved. Printed in the United States of America

1200

ISBN 0-574-06000-6

87 88 89 90 / 15 14 13 12 11 10 9 8 7 6 5 4 3 2 1

CONTENTS

FOREWORD

This book is intended for young writers—whether they are young in years or in writing experience. Its compact size is designed to make it easy to carry and use as a ready reference.

The young writer often has questions that need a quick answer: Which word is correct in this sentence? How can I organize this essay or letter? What is the correct spelling rule? This book will provide answers to such questions quickly and easily. The topics are arranged in alphabetical order. For example, spelling rules are found under "S." The index lists more specific information. Note, too, the "List of Words Commonly Confused" near the end of the book.

Whether for school or personal use, this book will be a helpful tool for solving all kinds of writing problems.

ABBREVIATIONS

An abbreviation is a short form of a word. For example, *Mr.* is an abbreviation for the word *Mister*. Most abbreviations end with a period.

In formal writing and in most writing that you do for school, it is best not to use abbreviations. There are certain cases, however, where you may use abbreviations.

1. You may use these abbreviations before names: *Mr.*, *Mrs.*, *Ms.*, *St.* (saint), *Dr.* (doctor).

   Mr. Allman
   St. Paul
   Dr. Susan Jones

2. You may use certain abbreviations after names.

   Thomas Walker, Jr.
   Susan Jones, M.D.
   Bruce Hill, Ph.D.

3. You may use abbreviations when writing the time.

   9 A.M.   3 P.M.

4. You may use abbreviations when writing dates.

   10 B.C.   (B.C. = before Christ)
   A.D. 476   (A.D. = *anno Domini*, "in the year of the Lord")

5. Names of organizations are often abbreviated. (Only the first letters of the words in their names are used.) Note that the abbreviations for the names of many organizations are written without periods.

   FBI   NATO   AFL-CIO
   NAACP   UN   IRS

6. Official names of states may be abbreviated when they are part of an address. Note that they are written without periods.

    155 North Wacker Drive
    Chicago, IL 60606

There are certain places where you should be careful not to use abbreviations.

1. Do not abbreviate parts of addresses when you write them in sentences.

   Correct: I live on Harmon Street, in Long Lake, New York.

2. Do not abbreviate names of months and days when you write them in sentences.

   Correct: I was born on Sunday, October 17, 1971.

ACTIVE AND PASSIVE VOICE

This is a sentence in the *active* voice:

   Sue hit the ball.

This is a sentence in the *passive* voice:

   The ball was hit by Sue.

In the first sentence Sue is doing the action. The word *Sue* is the subject.

In the passive voice the person or thing receiving the action is the subject. In the second sentence the ball is receiving the action. The word *ball* is the subject.

When telling a story or writing about what happened, you should use the active voice most of the time.

Weak: The story was told by José.
Better: José told the story.

There are some times when the passive voice will sound better.

1. If the person or thing receiving the action is more important than the person or thing doing the action, use the passive.

    The President was shot by a man in the crowd.

2. If you are not sure who or what did the action, use the passive.

    The school was built in 1942.

3. If you do not wish to mention who or what did the action, use the passive.

    While you were gone, Mother, a dish was broken.

ADDRESSES

There are two correct ways to write an address.

When writing an address on an envelope or in a business letter, use this form:

    29 West Main Street
    Lawrence, NJ 08852

Notice that a comma is used between the city and the state. No comma is used before the ZIP code. The official abbreviation of the state is used without periods. No other word is abbreviated.

The table shows two ways of abbreviating states and certain other territories. The first way is authorized by the U.S. government with ZIP code addresses. The second form is found in many lists, tables, indexes, bibliographies, or footnotes. Notice that Alaska, Guam, Hawaii, Idaho, Iowa, Maine, and Ohio are spelled out.

AL	Ala.	KY	Ky.	OH	Ohio
AK	Alaska	LA	La.	OK	Okla.
AZ	Ariz.	ME	Maine	OR	Oreg.
AR	Ark.	MD	Md.	PA	Pa.
CA	Calif.	MA	Mass.	PR	P.R.
CO	Colo.	MI	Mich.	RI	R.I.
CT	Conn.	MN	Minn.	SC	S.C.
DE	Del.	MS	Miss.	SD	S.Dak.
DC	D.C.	MO	Mo.	TN	Tenn.
FL	Fla.	MT	Mont.	TX	Tex.
GA	Ga.	NE	Nebr.	UT	Utah
GU	Guam	NV	Nev.	VT	Vt.
HI	Hawaii	NH	N.H.	VA	Va.
ID	Idaho	NJ	N.J.	VI	V.I.
IL	Ill.	NM	N.Mex.	WA	Wash.
IN	Ind.	NY	N.Y.	WV	W.Va.
IA	Iowa	NC	N.C.	WI	Wis.
KS	Kans.	ND	N.Dak.	WY	Wyo.

When writing an address in a sentence, use commas between the parts, as in this example:

I live at 29 West Main Street, Lawrence, New Jersey.

No abbreviations are used in the sentence.

ADJECTIVES

An adjective is a word that modifies or tells more about a noun or a pronoun. The words in italics are adjectives: *old* man; *tasty* food; *quiet* lake.

Adjectives tell **size:**   a *small* boy.
They also tell **color:**   a *red* hat.
They also tell **quality:**   a *sad* story.

Notice that adjectives often come before the noun they modify. They can also come after the verb *be*.

Angela is *kind*.

This book is *interesting*.

When you write descriptions, use specific adjectives, not general ones. A specific adjective gives more information than a general adjective, as these examples show:

Specific: That's a *warm* coat.
General: That's a *good* coat.

Some adjectives are used so much that they have lost much of their meaning: *nice*, *awful*, *wonderful*, *fantastic*, *great*, *good*. Avoid using such adjectives in your writing. Use specific adjectives instead.

ADVERBS

An adverb is a word that modifies or tells more about a verb.

Adverbs tell **how**:	Watch *carefully*.
They also tell **when**:	He called *recently*.
They also tell **where**:	Go *outside*.
They also tell **how often**:	She *usually* runs home.
They also tell **to what degree**:	It was *very* hot.

One way to tell adverbs is to look for the ending *–ly*. Many adverbs end in *–ly*; not all do so, however.

It is sometimes difficult to tell whether you should use an adverb or an adjective after a verb. This is often true with verbs such as *look*, *taste*, *feel*, *smell*, and *sound*. These verbs can be either linking verbs or action verbs. Try to remember this rule: If the word following the verb describes the noun subject, use an adjective. The verb is a linking verb and takes an adjective.

Correct: The tea tastes *bitter*.
Everyone on the team looked *strong*.
The rose smells *sweet*.

When the word following the verb describes the verb's action, use an adverb.

Correct: He looked *quickly* at the test.
The dog smells *carefully* along the ground.
Incorrect: She played *good* today.
Correct: She played *well* today.

It is important to remember that *good* is an adjective, *not* an adverb. It is never used to tell about a verb. Always use *well*, not *good*, to describe action.

AND

And is a conjunction. It is used to join words, groups of words, or short sentences that are closely related.

> The dog *and* the cat fought.
>
> We looked in the house *and* in the yard.
>
> We sent twenty invitations, *and* we received ten responses.

Keep in mind these suggestions about using *and* in your writing.

1. You should use *and* only occasionally to begin a sentence. When too many sentences begin with *and*, your writing sounds childish.

2. If you join two sentences with *and*, use a comma before the *and*, as in the third sentence above.

3. Do not overuse *and* in your writing. If you have used it to join several sentences, see if you can combine the sentences in different ways. Below are some examples illustrating this point.

Weak	Better
It began to rain, and I went home.	After it began to rain, I went home.
I was late to school, and I had to make up the time.	Because I was late to school, I had to make up the time.
She is my teacher, and I know you will like her.	She is my teacher; I know you will like her.

ANNOUNCEMENTS

When you make an announcement, you tell about something that will happen. You might make an announcement in your classroom: "The decorating committee will meet after school today." You might give your announcement over the school's public address system: "The trip to the zoo has been postponed because of bad weather." You might also put an announcement on a flyer or a piece of paper, like this:

```
STAMP CLUB meets Monday, February 3
    in room 316, 3:00-4:00 P.M.


       COLLECTING ANIMAL STAMPS

  An illustrated talk by Marian Wilkins

           Anyone may attend.
  Learn about an interesting hobby.
     See some beautiful stamps.


              REFRESHMENTS
```

When you are giving an announcement, keep these suggestions in mind:

1. Give full information: day, date, place, beginning and ending times, what will happen, who is sponsoring the meeting, who is invited.

2. Prepare the announcement with the audience in mind. Be sure the announcement includes information that will interest your readers or listeners.

3. Use language that your audience will understand. Short sentences are easier to understand and remember than long ones.

4. Be sure the announcement is correct in its form. Avoid slang. Check your spelling.

If you write an announcement that will be posted or handed out, make sure it looks attractive. Put the most important information in the center of the page. Use large letters and numbers that can be read easily. Leave space between the parts of the announcement.

If you give the announcement aloud, begin by telling who should listen: "Anyone interested in stamps or stamp collecting should attend the next meeting of the Stamp Club. . . ." Repeat the important information, since your listeners might not have been paying attention when you first mentioned the time, place, or date.

ANTECEDENTS

An antecedent is the word to which a pronoun refers.

antecedent   pronoun

Sonia   left   her   book   here.

antecedent   pronoun   pronoun

Everyone   should   bring   his   or   her   lunch   tomorrow.

Keep these rules in mind about the use of antecedents in your formal writing.

1. Make sure every pronoun has a definite antecedent.

   Incorrect: They don't have freedom of speech in the Soviet Union.

   Correct: The Soviet people do not have freedom of speech.

2. Make sure the antecedent is clear.

   Unclear: I asked Tom to come. I also invited Bill. He can't be there.

   Clear: I asked Tom to come. I also invited Bill. Bill can't be there.

3. Words that end in –*one* and –*body* (like *everyone*, *some-body*) are considered singular. They should take singular pronouns.

   Incorrect: *Everyone* should bring *their* English books tomorrow.

   Correct: *Everyone* should bring *his* or *her* English books tomorrow.

These rules are not as important when you are speaking or writing informally. For example, many educated people will say, "Does everyone have their notebooks ready?"

(You can find additional information in the section called PRONOUN AGREEMENT.)

APOSTROPHE (')

The apostrophe is a mark of punctuation that has two important uses:

1. To show ownership or possession.

2. To show where letters have been left out.

There are three rules about showing ownership or possession using an apostrophe. In the following examples the owner or owners are italicized:

1. If the object or objects belong to only one person, place, or thing, the owner is singular. Show possession by adding an apostrophe and an *s* to the name of the owner.

    Peter's books (the books of *Peter*)

    the *city's* problems (the problems of the *city*)

    the *boss's* orders (the orders of the *boss*)

2. If the object or objects belong to more than one person, place, or thing, the owners are plural. If the name of the owners ends in *s*, show possession by adding an apostrophe:

    the *boys'* club (the club of the *boys*)

    the *dogs'* bones (the bones of the *dogs*)

3. If the object or objects belong to more than one person, place, or thing, but the name of the owners does not end in *s*, show possession by adding an apostrophe and an s:

    the *mice's* cheese (the cheese of the *mice*)

    the *children's* toys (the toys of the *children*)

This chart shows the rules with some examples.

Singular or Plural	Ending	Add	Examples
Singular	no *s*	's	my father's job
Singular	*s*	's	Mr. Jones's job
Plural	*s*	'	the girls' lockers
Plural	no *s*	's	the children's shoes

A few special cases of ownership or possession are noted here.

1. The plural form of a family name ending in *−s* shows possession by the addition of the apostrophe only:

   the Joneses' house (the house of the Joneses)

2. Some ancient proper names ending in *−us*, *−es*, or *−is* require only an apostrophe to show possession:

   Jesus' parables (the parables of Jesus)

   Moses' Laws (the Laws of Moses)

3. Some abstract nouns ending in *−s* and followed by the word *sake* take an apostrophe:

   for goodness' sake; for righteousness' sake

4. Never use the apostrophe with the words *yours*, *hers*, *his*, *theirs*, or *ours*. They are called possessive pronouns. They do not take apostrophes.

The apostrophe is also used to show where letters have been left out. The apostrophe makes these words contractions.

could not	couldn't	they are	they're
it is	it's	do not	don't

ARTICLES

The words *the*, *a*, and *an* are called articles. *The* is called a *definite article*. It refers to a particular person, place, or thing. *A* and *an* are called *indefinite articles*. They do not refer to a particular person, place or thing.

Definite: Give me the book (A particular book is meant.)
Indefinite: Give me a book. (Any book is meant.)

Use *a* before words that begin with a consonant sound. Use *an* before words that begin with a vowel sound. Remember to think about the beginning *sound*, not the beginning letter. Some words begin with a consonant letter but a vowel sound, like the word *honest*. The *h* is not pronounced. Use *an* before those words.

He is an honest man.

Some words begin with a vowel *letter* but a consonant *sound*. Use *a* before those words.

My father belongs to a union. (The *u* letter is pronounced like a *y* consonant.)

AUTOBIOGRAPHIES

An autobiography is the story of your own life. (A biography is the story of someone else's life.) Your autobiography should meet these tests:

1. It should tell the reader the important facts about your life—when you were born, where you were born, and what important events happened to you.

2. It should interest the reader by telling about important places and events in detail. Write your autobiography like a story with action in it. Do not just state the facts.

3. It should help the reader understand what you are like. Explain what people and events have had an influence on you.

In writing your autobiography, remember that you do not have to tell things you would rather keep to yourself. Tell only what you want others to know.

There are many ways you can write your autobiography. Here is one plan that works well:

1. Write an introductory paragraph that interests your readers. Begin by telling how you feel in general about your life so far. Do not begin by writing, "I was born on . . ."

2. Write a second paragraph about when and where you were born. Tell about your earliest memories. Give the reader a picture of what you were like when you were very young.

3. Write a third paragraph about your first years in school. Tell in detail about something important that happened to you.

4. Write a fourth paragraph about the present. Tell about your hobbies, your friends, your family, your teachers.

5. End by telling what you hope for the future.

B

BIBLIOGRAPHY

A bibliography is a list of the sources used in writing a book or report. The bibliography comes at the end of the book or report. There are many correct ways to write a bibliography. One correct form is shown on pages 15–16. Notice that all the items are arranged alphabetically by the author's last name. If the author is not known, then the title is used as the first part.

When you are writing a report using several sources, make out a bibliography card for each source. You can then arrange the cards in alphabetical order and write the bibliography. Here is how a bibliography card might look.

author, last name first

title underlined

place of publication, publisher, copyright

brief note about usefulness of work

Kohn, Bernice

Our Tiny Servants

Englewood Cliffs: Prentice Hall, 1962

A good introduction to the subject

BIBLIOGRAPHY

Magazine article: author's last name followed by first name; title of article in quotation marks; title of magazine underlined; date, page numbers

Daly, Thomas. "The Promise of Yeast." Scientific American, February 1978, pp. 37–45.

Book: author's name; title of book underlined; place of publication; publisher, copyright date	Kauler, Lucy; <u>The Wonders of Fungi</u>. New York: John Day, 1964.
Interview: name of person interviewed; date of interview	West, Jane. Personal interview. December 1, 1981.
Encyclopedia article: title of article quoted; title of encyclopedia underlined; volume number; copyright date	"Yeast." <u>Colliers Encyclopedia</u>, Vol. 23. 1981.

BOOK REPORTS

A book report tells about a book you have read. Writing the report helps you think about and understand the book. It gives your teacher useful information about your reading. It is also a way of sharing your reading with your classmates.

Plan your book report carefully. Be sure to follow any special instructions your teacher gives you. If you have trouble planning your report, use a plan like this one:

1. Begin with a short introductory paragraph that tells the important facts about the book (title, author, type of book). The first paragraph should also tell your general opinion about the book.

2. The second paragraph can be a summary of the book. If the book was a nonfiction or factual book, tell about the main ideas you learned. If the book was a fictional book or novel, tell the important parts of the story. Tell the

names of the main characters and what they were like. State the main events in the plot or story. And tell about the setting, the time, and the place of the story.

3. The third paragraph can be a criticism of the book. Ask yourself if the author achieved his or her purpose. At the end of this section you will find questions you can ask in criticizing both fiction and nonfiction. In writing your criticism avoid overused adjectives like *good*, *poor*, *boring*, *interesting*. Give your reader more specific information: It was a fascinating story, filled with suspense and horror.

4. Write a brief concluding paragraph. Explain whether or not other readers would like the book.

When you revise your book report, be sure you have underlined the title of the book. Also, the first word and all important words in the title should begin with a capital letter. This sentence shows correct punctuation: I really enjoyed reading The Faces of Courage.

Questions to Ask in Evaluating Books

In criticizing a book of nonfiction, ask these questions:

1. What was the author's purpose? Did the author achieve it?

2. For what kind of reader was the book written? Would such a reader understand the book?

3. Is the author's information accurate? Is the book up to date?

4. Does the book seem clear and understandable? Does the author use diagrams, illustrations, and pictures to make the ideas clear?

5. Is the book interesting to read?

6. Does the book include an index to help you find information? Is there a bibliography or a list of other books on the same subject?

In criticizing a book of fiction, ask these questions:

1. What kind of fiction book is it—science fiction, horror, fantasy, historical, realistic, mystery?

2. What was the author's purpose? Did the author achieve it?

3. Were the characters described clearly? Did the characters seem like real people?

4. Was the setting clearly described? Could you imagine being there?

5. Was the plot interesting? Was it easy to follow? Was there enough excitement to hold your interest? Did the events seem real to you?

BUSINESS LETTERS

A business letter is a letter you write to a person or company about business matters. You might write a business letter for a number of different purposes:

1. To tell your opinions about some important matter.

2. To tell a public official what you think should be done.

3. To order goods from a company.

4. To apply for a job.

5. To complain about something a company has done.

A business letter has several parts:

Heading:	your name and address
Inside address:	the name and address of the person or company to which you are writing
Salutation:	the greeting, like *Dear Sir or Madam*
Body:	the main part of the letter in which you state your message
Closing:	the expression, like *Yours truly*, that shows you are ending the letter
Signature:	the signing of your name

There are many acceptable forms for the business letter. One form that is often used is shown on page 20. Notice the important points of punctuation: no period used with the state abbreviation; a comma between the day and the year; a colon after the salutation; a comma after the closing.

heading

4431 Osage Street
Philadelphia, PA 19104
October 10, 1983

inside
address

President, Society of Illustrators
128 East Sixty-Third Street
New York, New York 10021

salutation   Dear Sir or Madam:

body

I am very much interested in becoming a
commercial artist. The art teacher at our
school told me that you have a pamphlet
available on how to prepare for this career.

I would very much appreciate receiving a copy
of this pamphlet. I understand there is no
charge.

This career is very important to me, and
your assistance would be much appreciated.

closing

Yours truly,

signature

Susan M. Walker

Susan M. Walker

Remember that your business letter must make a good impression. Use white, unlined paper. Use a one-inch margin on all sides. Skip a space between the parts of the letter. Be sure that spelling and punctuation are perfect. And read your letter aloud before you send it off. It should sound courteous, even when you are making a complaint.

Address the envelope so that it includes both your name and address and the name and address of the person or company to which it is being sent. A sample envelope is shown.

```
Susan M. Walker
4431 Osage Street
Philadelphia, PA 19104




                        President, Society of Illustrators
                        128 East Sixty-Third Street
                        New York, NY 10021
```

C CAPITALIZATION

Capital letters are used to begin each sentence and each proper noun. A proper noun is the name of a particular person, place, or thing—such as *Jane Smith*, *the University of Michigan*, *Lake Erie*. There are many fine points involved in using capital letters correctly. The important rules are listed on page 22–23, with an example for each rule.

Rule: Always capitalize—	**Example**
1. The first word of a sentence	Here is your tie.
2. The first word of a quotation	He asked, "Where are you going?"
3. The pronoun *I*	You know I care for you.
4. The first word and every other important word in title	I liked A Tale of Two Cities.
5. Geographical names	We visited Loon Lake in Adirondack Park in New York.
6. The words *north*, *east*, *south*, and *west* only when they refer to specific sections of the country	I like the South as a place to live.
7. Names of historical events and holidays, but not the seasons	I like Labor Day because it comes in the fall.
8. The names of races, nationalities, and religions	There are many Polish and German citizens living there. They belong to the Protestant, Catholic, or Jewish faiths.

Rule: Always capitalize—	**Example**
9. The names of business firms, schools, and organizations	I attend Roosevelt Middle School. My mother is an engineer at General Electric.
10. The brand names of products, but not the type of product	Here is a bar of Ivory soap.
11. The names of ships and monuments	We visited the Washington Monument.
12. School subjects that contain a proper name or that are followed by a Roman numeral	I am studying French and algebra; next year I will take Algebra II.
13. Words that show family relationships only when they are used as a name or as part of a name	I told Mother I liked Uncle Joe but my cousin annoys me.
14. A person's titles when used with that person's name. The word President is always capitalized when it means the head of the country.	I saw Senator Jones on television; the senator was talking with the President.
15. Words referring to God. Do not capitalize *gods* when the word means the spirits worshipped by ancient people.	Nature reveals God in all His glory. The Aztecs worshipped many gods.
16. A person's name; *Jr.* and *Sr.* when they follow a name.	I voted for Simon E. Walker, Jr.

CLAUSES

A clause is a group of words that has a subject and a predicate. Some clauses make sense by themselves. They can stand alone. They are called main or independent clauses. The following are examples of main or independent clauses:

> The game was over.
>
> We went to the snack shop.

Some clauses do not make sense by themselves. They cannot stand alone. They should be part of another sentence. They are called subordinate or dependent clauses. Here are two examples:

> After the game was over
>
> . . . which is on Main Street

You can make your sentences sound more mature by writing sentences with one main clause and one or more subordinate clauses.

Immature writing: The game was over. We went to the snack shop. The snack shop is on Main Street.

Mature writing: After the game was over, we went to the snack shop on Main Street.

CLINCHER SENTENCES

A clincher sentence comes at the end of a paragraph. It restates or "clinches" what has been said before. There is an example of a clincher sentence at the end of this paragraph:

Many of the pests that bother us the most can be controlled by their natural enemies. Cats, of course, can control rats and mice. Shrews eat mice and also many kinds of insects. Slugs and other insects are eaten by centipedes. The praying mantis eats almost anything it can catch. Ladybugs enjoy a tasty meal of aphids, scales, and mealy bugs. And wasps eat caterpillars and other insects. This biological control of pests pits one form of life against another.

A clincher sentence is most effective at the end of a long paragraph. You should not use a clincher sentence with a short paragraph or with every paragraph you write. Use a clincher sentence to remind your readers of an important point or to sum up what you have said.

COLON (:)

The colon is a mark of punctuation that looks like this : It has many special uses. The most important ones are these.

Rule: Use a colon—	**Example**
1. After the salutation in a business letter	Dear Sir:
2. In writing the time figures	4:25 A.M.
3. Between chapter and verse of the Bible	My favorite passage is John 3:16.
4. After the word *following* before a list	Please send me the following: salt, pepper, flour, and butter.

COMMA (,)

The comma is used to show a slight pause in the sentence. It helps the reader understand the sentence more clearly. The main uses of the comma are shown in the chart.

Rule: Use a comma—	**Model Sentence**
1. Between the day of the week and the date, and between the date and year.	1. The attack on Pearl Harbor occurred on Sunday, December 7, 1941.
2. Between the parts of the address when written in a sentence.	2. She lives at 20 John Street, Poe, Ohio.
3. After the salutation of a friendly letter.	3. Dear David,
4. After the closing of any letter.	4. Yours truly,
5. Between the items in a series. Do not use a comma after the last item.	5. You need ambition, good health, and honesty to succeed.
6. Between two main clauses joined by *and*, *but*, *or*, *yet*. Do not use a comma when the last part does not include a subject.	6. Smoking causes cancer, and cancer is a major cause of death.
7. After introductory words like *well*, *yes*.	7. Well, you really tried hard that time.
8. After a participial phrase that begins a sentence.	8. Realizing the car was moving, I stepped on the brake.

Rule: Use a comma—	**Model Sentence**
9. After a subordinate clause that begins a sentence.	9. After I finish school, I plan to travel.
10. Around words used in speaking to a person.	10. Your problem, my friend, is a big one.
11. Around words that interrupt the sentence.	11. The story, however, is a true one.
12. To separate an appositive from the rest of the sentence. An appositive is a phrase that explains and means the same as the noun it follows.	12. Our neighbor, Mrs. Hancock, took us to the play downtown.

COMPARATIVE AND SUPERLATIVE FORMS OF ADJECTIVES AND ADVERBS

An adjective tells more about a noun or pronoun. An adverb tells more about a verb. You can use adjectives and adverbs in comparing people and things.

Adjectives: John is *smart*.
He is *smarter* than I am.
In fact, he is the *smartest* boy in the whole class.

Adverbs: She runs *fast*.
She can run *faster* than I.
She runs the *fastest* of any member of the team.

When you compare two things, you use the *comparative* form.

> John is *taller* than Bill.
>
> This dress is *more attractive* than that one.

When you compare more than two things, you use the *superlative* form.

> John is the *tallest* boy I know. (He is compared with all the boys you know.)
>
> This dress is the most attractive of all. (The dress is compared with many dresses.)

Notice that the comparative form is made in two ways. You can add *−er* to the original adjective or adverb: kind, *kinder*; tall, *taller*. With longer words, you can use the word *more* before the adjective or adverb: intelligent, *more intelligent*; inspiring, *more inspiring*.

The superlative form is also made in two ways. You can add *−est* to the original: old, *oldest*; sweet, *sweetest*. Or you can use *most* before longer adjectives or adverbs: *most intelligent*, *most inspiring*.

There are two important rules to remember.

1. Do not use the superlative form to compare two things.

> **Correct:** I like both apples and oranges, but I like apples *better*.
>
> **Wrong:** I like apples and oranges, but I like apples *best*.

2. Do not use the two ways of forming the comparative or the superlative together.

Correct: This is the *sweetest* apple I've ever tasted.
Wrong: This is the *most sweetest* apple I've ever tasted.

(You will find additional information in the section called MODIFIER USAGE.)

COMPARISON AND CONTRAST

When you compare two persons, places, or things, you show how one is like the other. When you contrast two things, you show how they are different. Sometimes the word *compare* is used to mean "show how things are both similar and different."

Often in your school work your teacher will ask you to write a comparison or contrast. Here are some sample assignments of this sort.

"Compare the government of China with that of Japan."

"Compare the climate in Florida and in Maine."

"In some families both parents work full time. In other families only one parent works. Compare family life in these two situations."

Plan carefully before writing a comparison or contrast. List all the important information about the two things being compared. Suppose, for example, you are comparing Washington and Lincoln. You might make two lists like this:

Washington	Lincoln
born of wealthy family in Virginia	born of poor family in Kentucky
studied surveying	had no regular schooling; taught himself
was a major at age twenty	did many odd jobs— storekeeper, railsplitter
successfully led the army in the Revolution; had several defeats as well as victories	was a captain in a volunteer company in the Black Hawk War but did not see battle
chosen first President and unanimously re-elected	lost several elections; finally elected President
often criticized by other political leaders	often criticized by other political leaders
led country through first difficult years	led country through Civil War
gave famous Farewell Address	Gave many speeches, including famous Gettysburg Address

As you make those lists, put similar items across from each other. That will help make the similarities and differences stand out. There are several good ways to write the comparison and contrast. Here is one way you can try.

1. Write a short opening paragraph in which you explain what you are comparing.

2. Write a paragraph about the first person, place, or thing. Include the important points from your list.

3. Write a paragraph about the second person, place, or thing. Be sure to tell the ways in which the second is similar to or different from the first.

4. You may wish to end with a short concluding paragraph that tells whether these two things were more alike or more different.

COMPLEX SENTENCES

All sentences are made up of clauses. A clause is a group of words containing a subject and a predicate. Some clauses can stand by themselves. They are called main or independent clauses.

I ran down the street.

Some clauses do not make sense by themselves. They need to be part of a sentence. They are called subordinate or dependent clauses.

While I was running down the street . . .

A complex sentence is a sentence that contains one main clause and one or more subordinate clauses. Here are some examples of complex sentences with the clauses marked.

┌───────── subordinate clause ─────────┐   ┌──── main clause ────┐
1. While I was running down the street,   I saw a man hit a dog.

┌── main clause ──┐   ┌──────── subordinate clause ────────┐
2. I like a school   where there is good discipline.

Using a complex sentence is a good way of combining two or more short sentences. Here are some examples.

Two short sentences: I like living on a farm. There are many ways I can help my family.

One complex sentence: I like living on a farm because there are many ways I can help my family.

Two short sentences: Washington was a successful person. He knew how to overcome defeat.

One complex sentence: Washington was a successful person who knew how to overcome defeat.

COMPOUND SENTENCES

A compound sentence is a sentence made up of two or more main or independent clauses. Each clause has a subject and a predicate. Each clause could make sense alone.

┌── main clause ──┐   ┌──────── main clause ────────┐
I am hungry,   and I would like to eat right now.

There are three correct ways to punctuate compound sentences.

1. Use a comma between the main clauses when the main clauses are joined with *and*, *but*, *or*, *for*, *yet*.

   You may leave, or you may stay.

2. Use a semicolon if the main clauses are not joined with any conjunction or joining word.

   You may leave; you may stay.

3. Use a semicolon if the main clauses are joined by connecting words like *however*, *therefore*, *consequently*, *moreover*. Also use a comma after those connecting words.

   You may leave; however, it would be unwise.

Remember to use compound sentences only when the two ideas you wish to express are closely related and are of equal importance. If one idea is more important than the other, put the less important idea in a dependent or subordinate clause.

Effective use of compound sentence: I was tired, but I stayed up.

Less effective use of compound: I was tired, and I went to bed.

More effective sentence: Because I was tired, I went to bed.

CONCLUDING PARAGRAPH

When you write a long composition or essay, you may want to end with a special concluding paragraph. A concluding paragraph is a short paragraph that comes at the end of the composition. It helps the reader know that the composition is finished.

A good concluding paragraph will often sum up what has been said. It will bring all the main ideas together. For example, here is the concluding paragraph of a composition comparing Washington and Lincoln.

> As you can see, Washington and Lincoln were different in many ways. In one important way, however, they were quite similar. They led our nation with courage and honor through very difficult periods.

A good way to conclude an essay of opinion is to suggest what your readers might do about the topic being discussed. Here is the concluding paragraph of an essay about why handguns should be licensed.

> If you believe as I do that handguns should be licensed, write a letter to your senator or representative in Congress. There is now a bill being considered that needs your support.

If you have written a short composition, you may not need a separate concluding paragraph. You may end with your last main point.

Do not write childish endings like ''The End,'' or ''This is all I have to say.''

CONCRETE DETAILS

When you are describing something or telling a story, you should use many concrete details. A concrete detail gives specific information about what is being described or what is happening.

Here is a description without enough concrete details:

My mother seems like a very young person in many ways. I like her because she acts young without being childish or silly.

Notice how concrete details make the picture more vivid:

My mother seems like a very young person in many ways. Her bright smile gives her face a youthful appearance. Her daily exercises and balanced diet keep her looking youthful and trim. She says she can still wear her wedding dress. And her voice always has a lilt to it that makes me know she is not discouraged even when things are going badly. She also is young in her thinking. She changed political parties because her ideas about the economy have changed. She is young in spirit, but she is also mature. She thinks logically about problems and doesn't buy expensive things on impulse. And she has never embarrassed me by being childish or silly.

There are many kinds of concrete details you can use. You can give specific facts (''she doesn't buy expensive things on impulse''). You can mention specific examples (''she changed political parties''). You can mention specific sights, sounds, smells, tastes, and feelings (''her bright smile . . . looking youthful and trim . . . her voice has a lilt to it'').

Here is part of a story that is interesting because it has many concrete details.

I slowly pushed open the heavy door into my mother's study. My stomach felt all knotted, as if there were bands of wire all twisted inside.

"Ma—I uh—can I talk for a minute?" I knew I was biting my nails even as I was trying to talk.

She put down that big thick law book she is always reading. She smiled quietly, and her eyes lit up. Every time she sees me this light comes into her eyes, even though something may be wrong.

"Sounds like you have a problem. Come sit down. I'm tired of reading, anyway."

When you are telling a story, give many concrete details. Tell what people feel. Tell about their actions. Describe how things look and sound. And tell the words they say.

CONJUNCTIONS

Conjunctions are joining or connecting words. They are used to join words, phrases, and clauses. The two most important kinds of conjunctions are called *coordinating conjunctions* and *subordinating conjunctions*.

Coordinating conjunctions are used to join equal words, phrases, or clauses. The most important coordinating conjunctions are *and*, *but*, and *or*. *Nor*, *for*, *so*, and *yet* can also be used as coordinating conjunctions.

Here are examples of coordinating conjunctions.

To join equal words: He was thin *and* wiry.

To join equal phrases: We looked in the barn *and* in the attic.

To join equal clauses: We looked in the barn, *but* we could not find him.

Subordinating conjunctions are used to join two unequal parts of a sentence. One part is subordinate to or dependent on the other. Here are the most common subordinating conjunctions.

after, although, as, because, before, how, if, provided, since, than, that, though, unless, until, when, where, while

CONNOTATION OF WORDS

Words have both *denotations* and *connotations*.

The denotation of a word is its factual meaning. For example, the denotation of the word *home* is "a place where one lives."

The connotations of a word are the feelings associated with it. For most people the word *home* would have these connotations: a place of love and security; a place where I feel I belong; a special place where people accept me; a good place where all my family gather.

Not all words will have strong connotations. For example, there are not many feelings associated with the word *inch*. Words that affect feelings have the most connotations.

When you use such words, think about their connotations. Be sure that the word has the connotation you intend. For example, if you are describing someone who is attractively slender, don't call that person *skinny*. *Skinny* has a negative connotation. It means unattractively thin.

CONTRACTIONS

A contraction combines two words by leaving out one or more of the letters of one of the words. Here are some examples of contractions.

Original	Contraction
could not	couldn't
should not	shouldn't
will not	won't
do not	don't
cannot	can't
I have	I've
have not	haven't
I will	I'll
you will	you'll

Notice that the apostrophe is used to show where the letters have been left out. You may use contractions in your informal writing. Avoid using contractions when you are writing formal papers and speeches.

DATES

There are two correct ways to write dates.

In a business or friendly letter, write the date like this:

October 13, 1983

Use a comma between the date and the year. Do not use forms like 13th or 2nd. When writing the date in a sentence, use the same form. Be sure that the parts of the date are separated with commas.

I was born on February 15, 1970, in a small town in Ohio.

When only the month and the date are given, no commas are needed.

I was born on February 15 in a small town in Ohio.

Notice that the names of days of the week and of months are capitalized.

In 1984, Halloween comes on Wednesday, October 31.

DESCRIPTION

A description is a word picture. You can write a description of a person, a place, or an object. These suggestions should help you write a good description.

1. Begin by telling the main impression you have of the person, place, or object.

2. Organize the description in a clear and understandable way. Most descriptions follow a spatial order—for example, from top to bottom, left to right, far to near, inside to outside. You can also organize the description by telling what you noticed first and ending with what you noticed last.

3. Give many concrete details. A concrete detail (sometimes called a sensory detail) is a specific fact about what the thing looked like, smelled like, sounded like, felt like, or tasted like. (See section entitled CONCRETE DETAILS.)

Here is an example of a description that follows the suggestions given here.

main impression in first sentence

paragraph organized clearly from what is first noticed to what is last seen

many concrete sensory details

Our classroom was a place where everything was in order. You would notice first the desks all lined up in straight rows. Then you would be aware of the quiet. You would hear only the whispers of the teacher and a pupil talking quietly. On the bookshelves under the window you would see all the social studies books piled in even stacks. The books all faced the same way, with the dark blue spines all in a row. Finally, if you looked closely, you would notice that all the papers on the bulletin board were carefully attached with a thumbtack squarely in each corner.

(You will find additional information in the section called SENSORY IMAGES.)

DIALOG

Dialog reports the actual words used in conversation. The following is an example of dialog:

"Did you see my hat?" he asked.

"I think you put it on the table," his mother replied.

Use dialog in telling a story or in showing what a person is like. Dialog adds interest to a story.

The dialog on pages 41–42 presents several ways to show who is talking when you write dialog. Notice that the writer does not keep saying "he said," "she said." The dialog also shows you how to punctuate correctly when you are telling what people actually said.

Sample Dialog

question mark inside quotation

As soon as I saw Tom, I knew something was bothering him. "What's wrong?" I asked with a smile.

indent every time a new speaker speaks

"Nothing," he grunted.

divided quotation; second part begins with small letter

"I guess you'd rather not talk about it now," I answered, "but I would like to be able to help."

indenting shows that a different speaker is speaking; no need to say who is speaking

"Well, there was a problem at school today."

"Something serious?"

"I guess going to the principal's office is serious."

a third person speaks, so
she must be identified

Just then Sue came running in. "Mom," she shouted, "Do you know what happened to Tom today?" Then she saw Tom.

Tom speaks two sentences;
one set of quotation marks
used

He barked at her, "You don't have to tell. I'm saying it my own way."

DIRECTIONS

You can write two kinds of directions. You can give a person directions that will tell him how to get from one place to another. Or you can give a person directions that tell how to make something.

Directions to a Place

Here are some suggestions to keep in mind when you give directions to a place:

1. Think about the person receiving the directions. How much does that person know about your area? In what general direction will that person be coming? Does that person already have a printed map showing the major roads?

2. Begin with a general picture of the route and the time.

    You'll be traveling in a northeast direction. The trip is about 150 miles and will take about three and one-half hours.

3. Make the directions very specific. Give exact distances, if possible.

    Drive five miles after you make that left turn.

4. Mention important landmarks. A landmark is a building or some large object that can be seen easily.

   You will see a Civil War monument on the right side of the road. Turn left at the first stoplight past the monument. The road is called King's Highway, and there is a gas station on the right corner.

5. Draw a map or sketch to go along with your written directions.

Directions for Making Something

When you tell someone how to bake a cake or make a bookcase, you are giving directions for making something. These suggestions should help you:

1. Think about the person for whom you are writing. How much does that person know about what you are explaining? What tools and equipment does that person probably have?

2. Begin by telling what is to be made, how it can be used, and why it is useful.

3. Then tell the preparations that should be made before beginning the project. The preparations stage includes these matters: what skills are needed; what safety precautions should be taken; what tools or equipment is needed; what materials and supplies are needed.

4. Then tell the steps the person should take in making the project. Give the steps in the order in which they should be taken. Use signal words to make the steps clear: *first*, *next*, *then*, *following that*, *third*, *finally*.

5. Give very specific explanations. Tell the exact time that the cake should bake. Tell exactly how long and how wide the shelf should be.

6. Define or explain any terms that the reader might not know.

DOUBLE NEGATIVES

Words such as *none*, *not much*, or *not* are called negatives. Other words that are often used with a negative meaning include *never*, *no*, *nothing*, *hardly*, *scarcely*, *but*. Do not use two negatives when one will do. Here are some examples:

Double negative: Michael does*n't* have *nothing* to do.
Single negative: Michael does*n't* have anything to do.
                       Michael has *nothing* to do.

Notice that the word *but* is sometimes used as a negative. It is therefore better to avoid using the expression *can't help but*.

Incorrect: I can't help but believe you are lying.
Better: I can't help believing that you are lying.

E

END PUNCTUATION (. ? !)

Remember the three ways to punctuate the end of a sentence.

1. Use a period after a sentence that makes a statement.

    The lake is calm today.

2. Use a question mark after a sentence that asks a question.

    Where have all the boats gone?

3. Use an exclamation mark after a sentence that shows very strong feeling.

    I love this lake!

There are a few special points to keep in mind about these end marks.

1. When the sentence ends with a quotation, the period always comes inside the quotation marks.

    He said, "You are wrong."

2. When the sentence ends with a quotation that asks a question, the question mark goes inside the quotation marks.

    She asked, "Where are my books?"

3. Use a period, not a question mark, with an indirect question. An indirect question is a statement that tells what a person asked, but that doesn't use the person's exact words.

    He asked if he could go.

ENVELOPES

The correct form for addressing envelopes for both business and friendly letters is shown below.

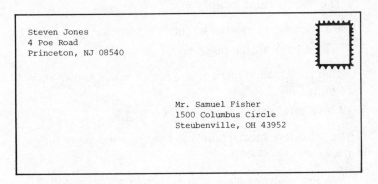

Be sure to write legibly when you address an envelope.

EXCLAMATION MARK (!)

The exclamation mark is used to end a sentence that shows very strong feeling. You can use a period if the feeling expressed is not very strong.

Very strong feeling: Stop thief!
Not very strong feeling: Stop, please.

When a sentence ends with a quotation that expresses very strong feeling, place the exclamation mark inside the quotation marks.

He shouted, ''There's the robber!''

EXPOSITION

Exposition is a type of writing. It is writing that explains. Here are several topics that show different kinds of exposition:

1. Explain how to do or make something. You explain a process.

2. Explain how two or more things are similar. You make comparisons.

3. Explain how two or more things are different. You make contrasts.

4. Explain what caused something to happen. You write a causal analysis.

5. Explain the effects of some event. You show the results.

6. Explain what a term or an idea means. You write a definition.

There are some general suggestions to keep in mind in writing exposition.

1. Think about your readers. How interested are they in your topic? How much do they know about your topic?

2. Plan the exposition carefully. Put your main points in the order that will make the best sense to your readers.

3. Begin the exposition by interesting your reader in the topic. Also tell your readers what you will explain. Here is an example of such a beginning:

> Would you like to earn some pocket money and also reduce your family's food costs? One interesting way to achieve both goals is to raise your own chickens. Let me explain how even a beginner can raise chickens and make some money.

4. The most important quality of good exposition is that it is clear. Explain all the special terms you use. Give many specific facts and examples. Make the organization clear by using signal words like *first*, *on the other hand*, *in the same way*, *the next kind*.

F

FIGURES OF SPEECH

A figure of speech is an expression that does not really mean what it says. It is used to make writing and speaking more interesting and more vivid. The most common figures of speech are explained below.

Simile: A simile is a comparison of two unlike things. The words *like* or *as* are always used in a simile.

The sky was like a gray blanket.

The driver's voice sounded like the barking of a dog.

Metaphor: A metaphor is a comparison of two unlike things. It does not use *like* or *as*. The comparison is only suggested.

The sky was a gray blanket.

The driver barked at me.

Personification: Personification is giving human characteristics to nonhuman things.

The heavens wept.

The trees bowed politely.

Hyperbole: Hyperbole is a statement that exaggerates in order to impress.

It must have snowed for about forty days straight.

There were a million people at your party.

FOOTNOTES

You use a footnote to tell where you found a certain fact, opinion, or quotation. When you write a report based upon books or articles you have to read, you should be sure to use a footnote in the following cases:

1. Always use a footnote when you have quoted a book or article.

2. Use a footnote if you use an opinion from a book or article, even if you do not quote directly.

3. Use a footnote to tell where you found a fact that is not widely known.

There are two places to put footnotes. You can put a footnote at the bottom of the page where you make that reference. The first example shows how to put the note at the bottom of the page. Or you can put all the footnotes together on a separate page at the end of your paper. The second example shows how a separate page might look. Notice in the first example that you use a raised number to refer to the footnote. If you put the footnote at the bottom of the page, then you should use the number 1 for the first note on each page, 2 for the second note on each page, and so on. If you use a separate footnote page, then you should number all the notes consecutively.

There are several correct forms for footnotes. The examples show a form that is widely used. Use that form unless your teacher wants you to use a different one.

Footnote at bottom of page:

Schlauch points out that many words from Native American languages came by way of the Spanish language.[1] Such words as *canoe*, *hurricane*, *potato*, and *chocolate* came to us by this route.

1. Margaret Schlauch, *The Gift of Tongues*, p. 97.

Footnotes on separate page:

Notes

1. Margaret Schlauch, *The Gift of Tongues*, p. 97.
   (footnote for a book)
2. Frank Trippett, "The Game of the Name," *Time*, August 14, 1976, p. 66.
   (footnote for a magazine article)
3. "Language," *Encyclopaedia Britannica*, vol. 16, p. 142.
   (footnote for an encyclopedia article)

FRAGMENTS

A fragment is a piece of a sentence that has been incorrectly punctuated as a sentence. Here are some examples of fragments (the fragment is in italics):

Since the weather was bad. We postponed the trip.

After waiting an hour for the bus. We decided to walk.

It was a tragic accident. *A depressing experience for all of us*.

She's not very dependable. *If you want my opinion*.

There are two ways to correct a fragment.

1. You can combine it with the sentence that comes before or after.

    After waiting an hour for the bus, we decided to walk.

2. You can make the fragment a sentence by changing it into a complete thought with its own subject and predicate.

    We waited an hour for the bus. We decided to walk.

When you are proofreading your own writing, check to be sure that you have not written a sentence fragment. Read each group of words that you have punctuated as a sentence. Be sure that each such group states a complete thought and has a subject and a predicate.

FRIENDLY LETTERS

When you write a friendly letter, be careful about the tone and the form.

The tone is the way your letter sounds. It should sound friendly and sincere. It should sound like your voice speaking.

Your friendly letter should also use good form. The correct form for a friendly letter is shown on page 53. Notice that the heading is the same as that used in a business letter. Use a comma after the salutation of the friendly letter. Notice also that only the first word of the closing is capitalized and that the closing is followed by a comma.

Friendly Letter

heading
Box 455
Long Lake, NY 12847
December 15, 1983

salutation
Dear Jeff,

body
I have some good news! My parents said that I can come for a short visit during the winter break. As my plans look now, our family will be driving to Tupper on December 26 and will be able to drop me off at your house that evening.

I know that your parents asked me to stay for the whole week, but my father and mother both have to be back at work on Monday. So we'll have to squeeze in the skiing, snow-mobiling, and ice-skating into that long weekend. That's better than no time at all, I guess.

Give my best wishes to your parents. It will be great seeing you again.

closing
Your snow-hungry friend,

signature
Bill

Bill

H   HYPHEN (-)

The hyphen has a number of uses.

1. Use a hyphen to separate compound adjectives that come before a noun.

    The before-school breakfast program included milk.

    The eighth-grade show was excellent.

2. Use a hyphen to separate two or more words or parts of words that together mean one thing. Here are some examples:

    Whole numbers or fractions written in two words: forty-four; one-quarter.

    Words that have the prefixes *co-*, *ex-*, *self-*, or *all-* added before the word: ex-wife; self-study; all-star.

    Proper nouns that have any prefix added before the word: anti-American; pro-Italian; mid-Atlantic.

    Compound words which are awkward or confusing unless they are divided by a hyphen: mother-in-law; re-enlist; runner-up.

3. Use a hyphen if you must divide a word at the end of a line. The most important rule in dividing a word is to divide it between syllables. A one-syllable word cannot be divided. If in doubt, consult a dictionary.

I

INDENTING

When a line of writing starts a few spaces in from the margin, it is indented. Indenting is one way to show a change in topic or new idea.

Every line you indent in your essay should be the same distance from the margin. This should be about one inch in handwritten papers and five spaces in typewritten papers.

Indent the first line of each paragraph. Your paper should look like this.

_____
_____
_____
_____
_____
_____
_____
_____
_____

Every time a new speaker begins, you must start a new paragraph. Indent the first line of the dialog even if the speaker only says one sentence.

"You give too much homework," Rebecca told her teacher.

"It helps you learn," he replied.

If you have a long quotation from some outside source, indent the entire quotation from the rest of the writing. A page with a long quotation would look like this:

INTRODUCTORY PARAGRAPH

An introductory paragraph is the first paragraph of a composition. An introductory paragraph is usually shorter than the rest of the paragraphs.

An introductory paragraph has two important jobs to do. First, it should try to arouse the reader's interest in the topic. Second, it should tell the reader what the main idea of the composition is. Here is an example of an introductory paragraph that does both jobs well:

> Our class is trying to raise money for a class trip. Several ideas have been suggested, but each has been found to be impractical. I would like to suggest a money-raising project that would also benefit needy families in our community.

If you have trouble beginning your composition, consider using one of these methods:

1. Begin with a question.

   Would you like to have a hobby that is both interesting and profitable?

2. Begin with a quotation from someone well known.

   In a recent speech the President talked about the importance of saving energy.

3. Begin with an anecdote or incident that relates to the topic.

   Last week one of the pupils in our school was injured while riding a bicycle to school. This serious accident illustrates the need for clearly marked bicycle lanes.

4. Begin with some important fact that relates to your topic.

   In an average week the typical teenager watches twenty hours of television.

5. Begin with a direct statement of your main idea.

   I believe our school should have a longer winter vacation so that we can save energy.

If you have a great deal of trouble getting started, begin with your first main paragraph. Then when you have finished your composition, go back and write an introduction.

Do not write an introduction that sounds childish or immature. Here is an example of such an introduction. It is too obvious.

   I am going to tell about how to make a bookcase.

INVITATIONS

Invitations can be formal or informal. A formal invitation to
a wedding or other celebration is often printed. If it is handwritten, it should look like this:

Mr. and Mrs. Lawrence Fitzsimmons
request the pleasure of
Mr. and Mrs. Walker's
company at dinner
on Thursday, April the twelfth
at eight o'clock

R.S.V.P.   325 Allen Lane
                           Shawmut

The letters *R. S. V. P.* stand for French words that mean
"Please reply."

An informal invitation uses the form of a friendly letter.
Just be sure that you include all the important information:
the kind of activity; the place; the day, date, and time; and
the kind of reply you want. An informal invitation is shown
on page 59.

If you wish to invite someone you do not know well to a
meeting of a club or organization, use a business letter form.
Give the same information.

Informal Invitation

heading
                                    4431 Osage Street
                                    Philadelphia, PA 19104
                                    October 14, 1983

salutation Dear Steve,

        I would like very much to invite you to my
        birthday party on Thursday, November 14.
        We're going to have dinner together with my
body   family and then go with all my friends to the
        hockey game. We'll have dinner around six
        o'clock. My father will give you a lift home
        after the game.

        I really hope you can come. Give me a call
        at 387-8430 to let me know if you can make
        it.

closing   Sincerely,

signature   *Bill*

                                    Bill

M   MANUSCRIPT FORM

When you write compositions or reports for school, be sure to use the correct form for your manuscript. Check to see if your teacher has any special rules.

The following rules apply to most manuscripts:

1. Use regular size (8½″ × 11″) white paper if you type. If you write, use regular lined composition paper (8″ × 11″).

2. Type or write in ink. If you write, use blue or black ink only.

3. Write or type on one side of the paper only.

4. Use appropriate margins. The length of your paper will affect the size of your margins. One-inch margins all around are usually satisfactory.

5. Put the proper heading on the first page. The heading usually includes your name, the school subject or class, and the date. Place this information in the upper right-hand corner of the first page, unless your teacher gives you other directions.

6. Place the title on the first page. Center the title on the first line. Skip a line between the title and the first sentence. Do not underline or put quotation marks around the title.

7. Number all pages except the first one with an Arabic number in the upper right-hand corner of the page.

8. Indent all paragraphs five spaces when you type and one inch when you write.

9. Be sure your paper is neat. Be sure your final paper does not include cross-outs or words added above the line.

MINUTES OF MEETINGS

The minutes of a meeting are the official record of what happened at the meeting. If you are asked to keep and write the minutes of a meeting you are attending, you should follow certain steps.

1. Keep careful notes. Note the date, time, and place of the meeting. Ask the people present to sign an attendance list.

2. Make careful notes of all the important actions taken. These are the actions that should be noted: reports by the officers of the organization; reports from committees; motions made and seconded; votes taken; names and responsibilities of people appointed to committees; announcements made about future events.

3. As soon as the meeting has adjourned, check with the person in charge about any matters that seem in doubt.

4. As soon as you can, make a good copy of the minutes.

Each group will have its own form for minutes. In general, most organizations use a form that includes the same basic elements listed below.

1. Use a heading like this:

    Minutes of the Stamp Club Regular Monthly Meeting, January 26, 1983.

2. State the time and place of the meeting.

3. List the names of all those present.

4. Number all the items you include.

5. Report only the decisions made and the actions taken. Do not include your personal opinion or your comments about actions.

6. Close the minutes with your name and title:

> Respectfully submitted,
> Alfredo Gonzales
> Acting Secretary

MODIFIER USAGE

A modifier is an adjective or an adverb. An adjective modifies or tells more about a noun or pronoun. An adverb modifies a verb.

The most important rules for modifier usage are given below, with correct and incorrect examples for each.

1. Compare two sentence parts correctly. In comparing two things, use the comparative form of the adjective. The comparative form ends in −*er* or uses the word *more*.

   Correct: He is the *taller* of the two boys.
   Incorrect: He is the *tallest* of the two boys.

2. Compare more than two sentence parts correctly. In comparing more than two things, use the superlative form. It ends in −*est* or uses the word *most*.

   Correct: Of the three boys, he is the *tallest*.
   Incorrect: Of the three boys, he is the taller.

3. Avoid double comparisons. Use *–er* or *–est* for short modifiers. Use *more* or *most* with longer words. Do not use *–er* and *more*, or *–est* and *most* together.

Correct: He is the *kindest* person I know.
Incorrect: He is the *most kindest* person I know.
Correct: She is the *most beautiful* person I know.
Incorrect: She is the *most beautifulest* person I know.

4. Use irregular adjectives correctly. Some adjectives are called irregular because they use special forms for the comparative and superlative. Here are some of the most common:

   bad, worse, worst
   good, better, best
   little, less, least
   far, farther, farthest

5. Use *well* and *good* correctly. *Well* is a confusing word. It has four different meanings, three as an adjective and one as an adverb.

Adjective: 1. to be in good health: I am *well*.
2. to be well dressed: You look *well* in that dress.
3. to be satisfactory: All is *well* with me.
Adverb: to do in an effective manner. He sings *well*.
Good is an adjective. You should not use it as an adverb.

Correct: She plays *well*.
Incorrect: She plays *good*.

(You will find additional information in the sections called ADJECTIVES and ADVERBS.)

N NARRATION

Narration is telling a story. A *narrative* is a story. A narrative can be a true or make-believe story. A make-believe narrative is called *fiction*.

If you are asked to write a narrative, you may find these suggestions helpful:

1. All good narratives involve conflict or struggle. The conflict may be between two people, between a person and a force of nature, or within a person.

2. An interesting narrative is focused. It tells a great deal about the most exciting moments. If you are telling a narrative about a weekend trip you took, do not waste time on the uninteresting parts. Get to the most interesting parts right away.

3. A good narrative has interesting characters. Choose one or two main characters. Tell their names, what they looked like, how they were dressed, how they felt and acted.

4. A good narrative has an interesting setting. The setting is the time and place of the action. Describe the setting so that it seems vivid to the reader.

5. A good narrative uses dialog. Dialog is the actual words of the characters. Show the characters speaking to each other. Use the dialog to show what they are like, what they are feeling, what they plan to do.

6. A good narrative ends in a way that seems convincing to the reader. Avoid trick endings or miracle endings that will make the reader feel cheated.

NEWS STORIES

A news story is a report of something that happened or an announcement of something that will take place. A news story is written in a special way.

The news story begins with a lead paragraph that gives all the important facts. Here is a lead paragraph for a sports news story:

> Central's championship football team lost their first game of the season to South, 17–14, with the winning margin provided by a field goal by Jason West, South's star kicker.

The rest of the news story is written so that the most important details are given first and the least important last.

There are two other important rules to keep in mind when writing a news story. First, keep the paragraphs short. A newspaper paragraph should ordinarily contain only two or three sentences. Second, use only the third person in writing the story. Do not refer to yourself as "I." Use your name instead. Do not address your readers as "you."

Remember that a news story should report only the facts. Your opinion should not be included.

NOUNS

A noun is the name of a person, place, thing, or idea. Here are some useful clues to help you identify nouns:

1. Nouns can be either singular (referring to one person, place, thing, or idea) or plural (referring to more than one). Most plural nouns end in −*s*.

2. Nouns are used as subjects or objects in sentences. As subjects, they often come first in the sentence: *John* is here. As objects, they often follow the verb: Bill hates *spinach*.

3. Nouns often follow the words *the*, *a*, or *an*.

4. Many nouns have special noun endings. Here are some common ones: *–ance*, *–dom*, *–eer*, *–er*, *–ful*, *–hood*, *–ism*, *–ist*, *–ity*, *–ment*, *–ness*, *–ship*, *–sion*, *–tion*.

Nouns can either be proper or common. A proper noun names a particular person, place, thing, or idea: *John Walker*, *Washington*, the *Rose Bowl*. Proper nouns are capitalized. A common noun names a general person, place, thing, or idea: *woman*, *city*, *game*. Common nouns are not capitalized.

OBJECTS

An object is a part of a sentence. There are direct objects and indirect objects.

A *direct* object is a noun or pronoun that receives the action of an action verb. The direct object is underlined in the sentences below.

I ate the pizza.

Hold the book carefully.

I miss you.

An *indirect* object is found in sentences that use verbs with a "give" meaning: *give*, *sell*, *tell*, *send*, *bring*, *ask*, *show*. These verbs take both an indirect and a direct object. The indirect object always comes before the direct object. The direct object tells what received the action of the verb. The indirect object tells to whom or for whom that action was taken. In the following sentences the indirect objects are marked "IO." The direct objects are marked "DO."

My mother told us a story.

He gave me a letter.

My uncle sent us a present.

ORGANIZATION

Organization in writing is the way ideas are related. An essay has a good organization if the reader can tell easily how the ideas are related to each other. An essay has poor organization if the ideas seem confusing and unclear in the way they are related.

There are several ways you can organize an essay.

1. **Chronological.** A chronological order tells things in the time order in which they happened. If you are explaining how to change a tire, you would probably use a chronological organization. You would tell the reader what to do first, then what to do next, and so on.

2. **Spatial.** When you use a spatial order, you tell about things in the way they are organized in space—left to right, outside to inside, top to bottom, near to far, and so on. If you are describing your room, you might use a spatial order. You would describe first what the walls look like, then what the floor looks like, and so on.

3. **Climactic.** A climactic order tells things in their order of importance—from least important to most important. If you are explaining why you think your school should be open in the evening, you would give your least important reason first and your most important reason last.

4. **Logical.** A logical order arranges ideas in a logical or reasonable pattern. For example, telling about the causes of a war and then telling about its effects would be a logical order.

Good organization comes when you follow a plan in your writing. Before you begin to write, make a list of your main ideas in the order in which you will discuss them. You can also make an outline showing your main ideas and the sub-headings for each.

When you make your plan, be sure to put all related ideas together. If you are discussing the advantages and disadvantages of opening school at night, put all the advantages together. Do not mix them with the disadvantages.

There are two good ways to make your organization clear to your readers.

One way is to explain to the reader how the essay is organized. You can often do that in the opening paragraph, as in this example:

> I think our school should be open in the evening for community use. In this essay I would like to explain the reasons for such an idea and then tell in detail how the plan will work.

The other way is to use transition words and phrases listed according to the order in which they are often used.

Chronological: *first, next, second, then, following, finally*

Spatial: *at the top, inside, from a distance, near the bottom*

Climactic: *to begin with, one reason, a more important, the most serious, the most important*

Logical: *on the other hand, another point, a related issue, as a result, in this connection*

(You will find additional information in the section called TRANSITIONS.)

OUTLINES

Before you begin to write, plan what you think you wish to say. One way to plan is to make an outline.

As you think about the topic you have chosen, decide on your main ideas. Suppose, for example, you have decided to explain why terriers make good house pets. You know you want to make three main points: they are easy to train, they have good dispositions, and they do not need much care. Those three main points become the main headings of your outline.

Terriers as House Pets
 I. Training
 II. Disposition
 III. Care

Now think about the details you wish to include under each main point. Those details become the subheadings of your outline, like this.

Terriers as House Pets
 I. Training
   A. Learn quickly
   B. Do not forget
 II. Disposition
   A. Friendly
   B. Good with children
 III. Care
   A. Feeding
     1. Food
     2. Vitamins
   B. Exercise
   C. Grooming

Notice that under "Feeding" the writer has added two sub-points. If your teacher wants you to submit your outline with your paper, be sure it has the correct form. Note these points about the form:

1. Place the title above the rest of the outline.

2. Use Roman numerals for your main headings, capital letters for subheadings, and Arabic numerals for next subheadings.

3. Indent all subheadings so that they line up with each other.

4. Put a period after each letter or numeral. Capitalize the first word.

5. Do not use the words *introduction* or *conclusion*. Those are not ideas. They are divisions of your paper.

6. Do not have only one subheading. Logically you cannot divide something into one part.

P PARAGRAPHS

A paragraph is a group of related sentences. The first word in every paragraph is indented. Teachers will often use these symbols to show paragraph errors:

¶   you should have begun a new paragraph here

No ¶   you should not have begun a new paragraph here

As you write your essay, you should begin a new paragraph when you wish to discuss a new idea. You should end the paragraph when you have finished discussing that idea. When you are proofreading your essay, check to be sure you have made good decisions about where paragraphs begin and end.

The main paragraphs of your essay are called developmental paragraphs. A good developmental paragraph has unity, coherence, and full development.

Unity means that the paragraph has a sense of "oneness." All the sentences are about the same general idea. No unrelated ideas are included.

Coherence means that the paragraph seems to stick together. The reader can easily tell how a sentence is connected to the one ahead and the one that follows.

Full development means that the main idea of the paragraph is explained with many facts, details, and examples. A thin paragraph is one that is not fully developed. The writer has not explained enough. In general your main paragraphs should be 50–75 words in length. If your paragraph has fewer than fifty words, it probably is not fully developed.

PARAGRAPH DEVELOPMENT

The main paragraphs of an essay are called the *developmental paragraphs*. They are the paragraphs that explain or develop your main ideas. These paragraphs should be fully developed. They should give the reader enough facts, details, and examples to understand your main idea.

There are several useful ways to develop your main ideas.

1. *Give specific facts and details.* Suppose your main idea is this one: Our town offers many advantages to businesses. You could develop that main idea by giving specific facts and details about the roads, the tax system, and the police protection.

2. *Give reasons.* A reason is a statement about why something should be done or why something is good or bad. You could use reasons to develop this main idea: I think our community should have a youth center. You would tell the reasons: it would reduce juvenile crime, bring young people together, and so on.

3. *Tell the steps or stages.* If you are telling someone how to do or make something, you would probably develop the main idea with the specific steps in the process.

4. *Give an example.* An example is a specific instance of the main idea. Suppose you are arguing that older people should not be forced to retire. You could give several examples of older people who are still working effectively.

There are many other ways to develop a paragraph. Those four are the main ones you will probably use in your writing. And often, of course, you will use two or more methods in developing one main idea. For example, if your main idea is how a youth center could reduce crime, you might give both reasons and examples.

PARALLELISM

Parallelism is using similar grammatical structures to express facts or ideas that are equal.

Parallel: I like swimming, fishing, and hunting.
Not Parallel: I like swimming, fishing, and to hunt.

The second example is not parallel because it uses two *–ing* words and an infinitive to express three closely related ideas.

PARENTHESES ( )

A parenthesis is a mark like this (or like this). The plural form is parentheses. These are parentheses: ( ).

Parentheses are used to enclose words or phrases that are not closely related to the rest of the sentence. Notice these examples:

The diagram (see Figure 2) shows how the wires should be connected.

The President (and you must remember I didn't vote for him) has really been doing an effective job.

Do not overuse parentheses. Commas and dashes are often more appropriate for setting off unrelated expressions.

PARTICIPLES

A participle is an adjective made from a verb. The participle is made from the *–ing* form of the verb or the *–en* or *–ed* form of the verb. Here are some examples of participles:

The *twisted* oak was bare of leaves.

The *falling* snow covered the trees.

Sometimes the participle is used with other words to make a participial phrase. The participial phrase is used as an adjective. The participial phrase is underlined in the sentences below.

<u>Seeing the bus leave</u>, I shouted to the driver.

<u>Hidden from view</u>, the robber waited nervously.

The poor dog <u>tied to the tree</u> looked hungry.

Beethoven, <u>stricken with deafness</u>, still composed great symphonies.

When you begin a sentence with a participial phrase, be sure that the main part of the sentence begins with the word to which the participle refers. If a participial phrase is not followed by its subject, it is said to dangle. Here are some examples of dangling participles:

Hoping to see you soon, this letter will now close.

(The letter isn't hoping.)

Running down the street, a bus hit a jogger.

(The bus wasn't running.)

There are two ways to correct a dangling participle. You can change the participial phrase to a clause by adding a subject and predicate, as in this example.

> While the jogger was running down the street, a bus hit him.

Or you can keep the phrase as it is and begin the main part of the sentence with the subject of the phrase.

> Running down the street, a jogger was hit by a bus.

PERSUASION

Persuasion is writing or speaking that tries to convince an audience to believe something or to take some action. Here are some topics that would be used in a persuasive essay:

> Why we should outlaw handguns.
> Why the _____ car is the best economy car.
> Why I believe the President made a wise decision about taxes.
> Why we should have longer vacations.

These suggestions should help you write good persuasive essays:

1. Think about your audience. How much do they know about the topic? What opinions do they probably have? What arguments will they most likely accept?

2. Plan the essay carefully. Think of all the reasons for your position. Get all the facts you can to support these reasons. A good organization for a persuasive essay will put the

strongest reason last. The next strongest reason comes first. The beginning and ending of the essay are the parts the reader remembers best.

3. Use reasons that will make sense to your readers. For example, you would stress the recreational opportunities of a youth center when writing for other students. You would stress the effect on delinquency when writing for parents.

4. Support your reasons with facts, examples, and quotations from experts. The more evidence you can provide, the more your readers will be ready to accept your reasons.

5. One good way to end the persuasive essay is to tell your readers what they should do next if they accept your idea.

PHRASES

A phrase is a group of related words. A phrase is used as part of a sentence. It cannot stand alone as a sentence. There are three main kinds of phrases.

1. *Prepositional phrase*. A prepositional phrase begins with a preposition. It is most often used as an adjective or adverb in the sentence.

Adjective prepositional phrase: The box *on the table* contains your gift.

Adverb prepositional phrase: He put the box *on the table*.

2. *Participial phrase*. A participial phrase begins with a participle. A participle is a verb form that usually ends in *–ing* or *–ed*. The participial phrase is most often used as an adjective.

   The dog *tied to the tree* is in pain.

   Feeling upset, he left suddenly.

3. *Infinitive phrase*. An infinitive phrase starts with the infinitive form of the verb. The infinitive form begins with *to*. The infinitive phrase has a number of uses.

   Noun: I like *to swim*.

   Adjective: That's the way *to do it*.

   Adverb: It is easy *to do*.

PLAYS

A play tells a story by showing what the characters do and say. A one-act play is a drama that takes place in one act. It focuses on one important action that affects people. If you would like to write a one-act play, you might find these suggestions helpful in thinking about the plot. The plot is what happens in the play. It is the action and events of the play.

1. Begin by thinking about a main character. Choose an interesting character, one whom you know well. The character can be real or fictional.

2. Think of some conflict that your character would be involved in. A conflict is a struggle between two people, or between a person and nature, or within one person.

3. Think about some opposing force that would be involved in the struggle, another character who would oppose the main character.

4. Think about the climax of your play. The climax is the place in the plot where the main conflict is decided. The climax is usually a time of intense struggle and conflict. It occurs near the end of the play.

5. Think about a few events that might lead up to the climax. Decide how the play would begin and how the conflict would develop.

Your notes about all these decisions become an outline for your plot. You are ready to write the one-act play.

Begin by listing your characters. Tell their names and identify each briefly, like this:

Susan: a teenager; slightly overweight, shy, and withdrawn

Bill: the new boy in town; quiet and sensitive.

Then tell the setting, the time, and the place. Describe it briefly, like this:

The scene is the classroom where the school paper is edited. The room has several tables and chairs, with papers and books scattered around. It is 4 o'clock on a winter afternoon. Susan, Bill, and Jerry are the only ones left. Mr. Walker, the sponsor, comes in and out but doesn't pay too much attention to what is being said.

Then show your characters speaking. If they take any important actions, tell what those actions are. This is the form to use:

> *Jerry*: I've about had it. I think I'll take off and finish up my page in the morning.
> (*Picks up books and coat, starts to leave, and then stops.*)
> Are you sure it's OK to leave you two alone?
>
> *Bill*: You just don't know me, do you? I'm never safe to leave alone.
>
> (*The two boys laugh. Susan is obviously embarrassed. Jerry leaves with a wave.*)

You can see that the play depends mostly on dialog to show what the characters are like and to tell what is happening. Write dialog that sounds natural. Read aloud what you have written. See if it sounds the way your characters would really talk.

POEMS

A poem is usually a short piece of writing that uses language in special ways to tell a story, describe a scene, or express strong feeling.

Some poems have a regular rhythm. When a poem has a regular rhythm, there is a pattern of stressed and unstressed syllables. Notice the rhythm of this line. (The stressed syllables are underlined.)

The <u>air</u> was <u>chilled</u> with <u>winter's</u> <u>frost</u>.

Not all poems have a regular rhythm. The lines are written as you might speak them. Here is a line that does not have a regular rhythm.

> Chalk-filled boards spoke of names and dates to be remembered.

Some poems use rhyme. When lines rhyme, their last sounds are the same. Here are two lines that rhyme.

> The air was chilled with winter's frost.
> The fawn was frightened, cold, and lost.

Not all poems use rhyme. This poem does not use rhyme in its opening lines.

> Chalk-filled boards spoke of names and dates to be remembered.
> But I had long forgotten what they meant.

All poems should use language in creative ways. Here are some points to keep in mind as you write your own poems.

1. Use specific and vivid nouns, verbs, and modifiers in your poems. Avoid vague words.

2. Use many sensory details. A sensory detail tells what something looked like, sounded like, smelled like, felt like, or tasted like.

3. Use creative comparisons. Help your reader visualize what you are describing by using original similes and metaphors. A simile is a comparison between two unlike things, using the words *like* or *as*. A metaphor is a comparison

that does not use *like* or *as*. The comparison is suggested or implied. Here are examples of both.

Simile: His voice was like a knife cutting through the air.

Metaphor: His voice knifed through the air.

4. Don't waste words. A good poem is concise. Every word counts.

PRÉCIS

A précis is a shortened summary of an article. If your teacher asks you to write a précis of an article keep the following suggestions in mind:

1. Skim the article first, just to get a general sense of what it is about.

2. Read the article more carefully. Make written notes of the main ideas and the important facts and details.

3. Write the précis by using the notes you have made. The précis should be about one-third the length of the original article. The main ideas and the facts should be in the same order in the précis as they are in the original.

When you write the précis, pretend you are the author of the original. Don't write ''This article says . . .'' or ''This author reports. . . .'' Just tell the main ideas and important facts as if you were writing the original.

Also, do not copy the words of the original. The précis should be in your own words, not the language of the original.

PREPOSITIONS

Prepositions are short words that show relationships.

Time relationship:	*after*, *before*, *during*, *on*, *since*, *until*
Place relationship:	*above*, *across*, *along*, *among*, *around*, *at*, *behind*, *below*, *beneath*, *beside*, *between*, *beyond*, *by*, *down*, *from*, *in*, *inside*, *into*, *rear*, *on*, *onto*, *out*, *outside*, *over*, *past*, *through*, *to*, *toward*, *under*, *up*, *upon*, *within*
Manner relationship:	*with*, *without*, *like*, *for*, *of*

Prepositions come before nouns and pronouns.

In formal writing, your teacher may suggest that you avoid ending sentences with prepositions.

Informal: Whom did you send the letter to?

Formal: To whom did you send the letter?

PRONOUNS

A pronoun takes the place of a noun. There are several important kinds of pronouns. These are the most important.

1. **Personal pronouns:** There are seven personal pronouns. They are *I*, *you*, *he*, *she*, *it*, *we*, *they*.

2. **Indefinite pronouns:** Indefinite pronouns refer to general or indefinite persons or things. Here are some common indefinite pronouns: *each*, *other*, *neither*, *either*, *anyone*, *anybody*, *anything*, *everyone*, *everybody*, *everything*, *someone*, *somebody*, *something*, *no one*, *nobody*, *nothing*, *both*, *few*, *many*, *several*, *others*, *none*, *some*, *all*, *any*, *most*.

3. **Relative pronouns:** *Who*, *whom*, *whose*, *which*, and *that* are called relative pronouns. They begin adjective clauses.

4. **Demonstrative pronouns:** The words *this*, *that*, *these*, and *those* are called demonstrative pronouns. They point out people or things.

PRONOUN AGREEMENT

A pronoun is a word that stands for a noun. The antecedent is the word which the pronoun stands for or refers to. When you write formally, be sure that the pronoun and its antecedent agree in number. When the antecedent is singular, the pronoun should be singular. When the antecedent is plural, the pronoun should be plural.

Most of the time you do not have any problems with this rule. The correct form sounds right to you.

     plural ant.   plural pro.
The *boys* brought *their* lunch.

   sing. ant.   sing. pro.
Bill brought *his* lunch.

There are two special problems, however, where you cannot trust "what sounds right."

1. These antecedents are singular and take singular pronouns: *each*, *either*, *neither*, *one*, *everyone*, *no one*, *nobody*, *anyone*, *anybody*, *someone*, *somebody*. Here are some examples for this rule.

   Does *everyone* have *his* or *her* lunch?

   Each of the boys brought *his* special pet to school.

   Neither of the girls knows where *her* father was born.

2. When two singular antecedents are joined by *or* or *nor*, use a singular pronoun. These examples are correct.

   Neither Tom nor Bill brought *his* coat.

   Either Sue or Helen will bring *her* tapeplayer to the party.

PRONOUN FORMS

Pronouns have three different forms, depending upon their use in a sentence.

Form	Use	Example
Subject	As a subject or after verb *be*	*He* is my friend. This is *he* speaking.
Object	As the object of a verb or preposition	I gave it to *him*. I like *her*.
Possessive	To show ownership	This is *my* book. This is *her* coat.

The two rules below call attention to common problems in pronoun form.

1. Use the subject form after the verb *be*. These examples are correct.

    It was *he* who broke it.

    It is *we* who are responsible.

    This is *she* speaking.

2. Be sure to use the object form in compound objects. A compound object is two words joined by *and* or *or*, both of which are objects of verbs or prepositions. When one or both of those words are pronouns, be sure to use the object form. These examples show the correct form.

    I gave the pie to Sue and *her*.

    They invited Tom and *me* to the party.

One good way to check with this second rule is this: drop the noun and the word *and* and use the form that sounds right. This example shows how to use this test.

Sentence: *She sent Bill and (I, me) to the office.*
Test: *She sent . . . me to the office.*

PRONOUN REFERENCE

When you use pronouns, be sure that they relate clearly and specifically to their antecedents. The antecedent is the noun to which the pronoun refers. Here are some special suggestions to keep in mind.

1. Repeat the noun if doing so makes the sentence clearer.

   Unclear: Keep your hand off the wall or it will get dirty.
   Clearer: Keep your hand off the wall, or the wall will get dirty.

2. Avoid using *it*, *you*, and *they* to stand for an indefinite person or group.

   Unclear: In olden times, you could be executed for disobeying the king.
   Clearer: In olden times, a person could be executed for disobeying the king.

Q QUOTATION MARKS (" ")

Quotation marks are punctuation marks that look like this: " " There are three main uses for quotation marks.

1. Quotation marks are used to set apart the titles of articles, poems, short stories, television programs, radio programs, and songs.

> My favorite patriotic song is "God Bless America."
> Read the encyclopedia article entitled "Plants in North America."

2. Quotation marks are used in writing reports when the words of another author are used:

> As Brown said in his report on fleas, "Get rid of those little things as soon as they come into the house."

3. Quotation marks are used to set apart the exact words of the speaker from the explanatory words. They are used in writing conversation.

> Sara said, "I am going to watch TV now."
> "No," said her mother, "you must wash your hair first."
> "But my teacher said to watch the news," Sara added.
> "Oh!" said her mother.

Notice the conversation between Sara and her mother. There are a set of special punctuation rules for writing conversation. When you wish to write conversation, check these punctuation rules.

1. Put quotation marks around the exact words of each speaker.

2. Start a new paragraph for each speaker.

3. When the explanatory words come before the exact words of the speaker:
   a. Use a comma after the explanatory words.
   b. Begin the quotation with a capital letter.
   c. Put the end punctuation inside the quotation marks unless the whole sentence is a question.

4. When the explanatory words come after the exact words of the speaker (as in sentences 3 and 4):
   a. Use a comma after the quotation if the quotation is a statement.
   b. Use a question mark or exclamation point after the quotation if the quotation is a question or an exclamation.
   c. Put all commas, question marks, and exclamation points that follow the quotation inside the quotation marks.
   d. Use a period after the explanatory words.

5. When the explanatory words come in the middle of a sentence that is a direct quotation (as in sentence 2):
   a. Put quotation marks around each part of the quotation.
   b. Put a comma inside the quotation marks after the first part of the quotation.
   c. Put a comma after the explanatory words in the middle of the sentence.
   d. Start the second part of the quotation with a small letter.

R REPETITION

Do not repeat words unnecessarily. Sometimes you may repeat for emphasis.

> I want to work with my *family* and for my *family*. My *family* counts with me.

You may also repeat a word to be clear.

> *Sue* and Helen both won, but *Sue* was a better player.

In all other cases, however, avoid repeating words. Use pronouns or synonyms to avoid repetition.

Unnecessary repetition: Libraries are important, but libraries have to be more than collections of books.

Better: Libraries are important, but they have to be more than collections of books.

REPORT WRITING

You are often asked to write a report for your school courses. When you write a report, you get information from books, magazines, and encyclopedias to help you explain the topic. Reports are also called *research papers*, *term papers*, or *library papers*. These suggestions should help you write a good report.

1. Choose a narrow or limited topic. Your report will be better if you have much information about a narrow topic. If your topic is too broad and covers too much then you will be able to give only a few details.

   Too broad: Nuclear energy
   Narrow: Disposing of nuclear waste

2. Use good sources. The sources are the books, magazines, and other materials you use to get the facts you need. The best sources are current and up to date. The best sources also give much information. Some encyclopedias are not good sources because they do not give enough information.

3. Take careful notes. The best way to take notes is to write them on $3'' \times 5''$ index cards. Put one source and one topic to a card. That will make it easy for you to arrange your notes.

4. Make an outline or plan for your paper before you write. Since the report is usually a longer paper, it is important to organize it clearly. A good outline will help you arrange your thoughts and write in a well-organized manner.

5. Use your own words, not the words of the original source. When you write your report, express ideas in your own language. Do not copy word for word from your source. The only time you should use words from the original is when you think those exact words are important. If you do use words from the original source, use quotation marks, like this:

> One critic called Steinbeck's novels "sentimental potboilers devoid of any lasting value."[1]

You also use a raised number, like the [1] above, to show that you will tell the source of that quotation.

6. Document your sources. As explained above, you should always tell what sources you used. When you tell your sources, you are *documenting* them. You document by using footnotes in the paper or at the end of the paper.

You also document by listing the sources you used in a bibliography.

7. Be sure your report is written well, with correct form. Write an effective introductory paragraph that arouses your readers' interest and states the topic of the report. Write well-developed main paragraphs that explain with much detail all the important ideas. Write a good concluding paragraph that summarizes. Check spelling, punctuation, and usage to be sure the paper represents your best work.

(You can find additional information in the sections on BIBLIOGRAPHY, FOOTNOTES, and OUTLINES.)

RUN-ON SENTENCES

A run-on sentence is an incorrect sentence. A run-on sentence combines two sentences into one but uses the wrong punctuation or no punctuation at all.

These are examples of run-on sentences.

I like cats I like dogs better. (No punctuation)
I like cats, I like dogs better. (Wrong punctuation)

SEMICOLON (;)

A semicolon has three main uses.

1. It joins two main clauses when no conjunction is used.

   My mother is Irish; my father is German.

2. It joins two main clauses when a conjunctive adverb is used between the clauses. These are the important conjunctive adverbs: *however, therefore, consequently, moreover, besides, instead, furthermore, hence, that is, nevertheless, for example, otherwise.*

   You are ill; therefore, you should stay at home.

3. It is used to separate items which already include commas. The semicolon makes the separation clearer.

   The visitors came from many cities: from Maplewood, New Jersey; from Akron, Ohio; from Poe, Illinois; and from Albany, New York.

SENSORY IMAGES

A sensory image is a group of words that gives a picture of what something smelled like, looked like, felt like, sounded like, or tasted like. Sensory images are very useful when you tell stories or write descriptions.

Sensory images are best when they give many specific details. Notice the sensory images in this passage. They are printed in italics.

The air was clear—but freezing cold. It stung my face *like a thousand sharp needles*, made my nose so *cold that it seemed to be on fire*. But I drank it in, like *cold refreshing water*—glad to be away from the *stuffy sweltering* air of the cabin.

There are several ways you can make sensory images part of your sentences. The examples below show some ways that are effective.

1. **Sensory verbs:**   the fire *crackled*

2. **Sensory modifying words:**   the *rough*, *worn* bark of the tree

3. **Prepositional phrases:**   The baby's skin was *like creamy milk.*

4. **Participial phrase:**   *Growling*, *snarling*, *gnashing* his teeth, the dog stood ready to charge.

5. **Clause:**   *When the fire burst into bright red flickering flames . . .*

SENTENCE STRUCTURE

Sometimes you will be told that you have an error in *sentence structure.* You probably have made one of the following mistakes.

1. *Fragment.* You punctuated a piece of a sentence as if it were a complete sentence.

   Incorrect: While I was waiting for my mother. I saw an accident.

   Correct: While I was waiting for my mother, I saw an accident.

2. *Run-on sentence*. You have combined two sentences incorrectly.

Incorrect: He is a good team member, he cooperates well.

Correct: He is a good team member; he cooperates well.

3. *Dangling participle*. You began a sentence with a participle but did not follow it with its subject.

Incorrect: Waiting at the airport, a terrible accident happened.

Correct: Waiting at the airport, I saw a terrible accident.

4. *Stringy style*. You have strung together many short clauses.

Stringy: We went to the shore for a vacation, and we had a wonderful time, but my brother got a bad sunburn, and he had to be treated by the doctor.

More mature: We had a wonderful time on our vacation at the shore. Unfortunately, my brother got a bad sunburn, which needed medical attention.

5. *Simple style*. You use too many short simple sentences.

Too simple: I like pizza. It's spicy. I like the melted cheese. It's a tasty snack.

More mature: I like the hot spices and melted cheese of tasty pizza.

6. *Sentence parts separated*. In general, you should avoid separating parts of the sentence that are closely related.

Awkward: The hungry bears, after they had been wakened too soon from their hibernation by an early spring, became aggressive.

Better: Wakened too soon from their hibernation by an early spring, the hungry bears became aggressive.

7. *Did not use parallel structures*. In general, use the same kind of grammatical structure for two or more related ideas.

Lacks parallel structure: I like to visit the mountains *to ski* and *for snowmobiling*.

Uses parallel structure: I like to visit the mountains *for skiing and snowmobiling*.

SENTENCE TYPES

Sentences can be grouped in two ways. Sentences can be grouped according to the meaning or feeling they express.

1. **Declarative sentences:** They make a statement and end with a period.

   The book was exciting.

2. **Interrogative sentences:** They ask a question and end with a question mark.

   Is that book exciting?

3. **Imperative sentences:** They make a request or give a command. The subject *you* is understood. They end with a period.

> Please hand me that book.
>
> Close the door.

4. **Exclamatory sentences:** They show very strong feeling and end with an exclamation mark.

> He's a liar!

Sentences can also be grouped according to their form. Form involves the type and number of clauses used. There are three main kinds of sentences: simple, compound, and complex. This chart shows the three types and the kinds of clauses they use.

Type of Sentence	Number of Main or Independent Clauses	Number of Subordinate Dependent Clauses
Simple	1	0
Compound	2 or more	0
Complex	1	1 or more

Occasionally you will use a special kind of sentence called a compound-complex sentence. It has two main clauses and one or more subordinate clauses.

One way to make your sentences sound more mature is to vary the sentence type. Do not use too many simple or compound sentences. Complex sentences sound more mature.

SLANG

Slang is a type of informal language. It consists of words and phrases that are very popular for a short time and are then forgotten. You and your friends may speak to each other in slang words that other people do not understand. Others may use slang words that you have never heard.

Slang should never be used in writing except when you are writing a dialog in which people speak in slang.

> Frankie found Timmy in the hall. "Have you seen the chick?" he asked.
>
> "Cool it," answered Timmy. "I think she's a square."
>
> "That's okay with me," responded Frankie. "I dig her."

Slang words are labeled in the dictionary. If you have a question about a word, check to see if the dictionary marks it "slang" or "informal English."

SOCIAL NOTES

There are many occasions to write a social note to someone. These are the three common types of social notes:

1. Invitations for a party or a visit.

2. "Thank you" notes after you receive a present.

3. "Bread-and-butter" notes after you stay at someone's house.

Social notes are usually written by hand. You should use your best handwriting so the person can read your note easily. In writing notes that thank people, try to say something specific about the gift or the visit. That way the person who gets the note will know that you appreciate the gift or the hospitality.

Social Note

heading

> 20 Stowe Road
> Toronto, Ohio
> January 8, 1983

salutation   Dear Mrs. Britt,

Thank you for inviting me to your house last weekend. Jeannie and I had a good time.

It was nice of you to take us rollerskating on Saturday. You must have guessed that I had not done much rollerskating before this trip, but I think I will go again. My mother says that she will take me to the rink.

Mom also asked if you would share your special pancake recipe with her. Perhaps when Jeannie comes to visit me in March she can bring it with her. I'm looking forward to her visit.

closing   Sincerely,

signature   *Elaine*

                                 Elaine

SPELLING

Correct spelling is important. Follow these suggestions to become a better speller.

1. Become aware of and concerned about your spelling. Always check your writing to be sure the words are spelled correctly.

2. Use your dictionary for any words about which you are uncertain.

3. Keep your own list of misspelled words. Write the correct spelling only, not the incorrect one. Put a check mark next to a word each time you misspell it. In that way you will know the ones you have to study most of all.

4. Use a good method for studying words. See the word, say it, spell it aloud, write it, check it.

5. Learn the important spelling rules. Most rules have too many exceptions to be of any use. The important rules are summarized on pages 100-102.

6. Memorize words commonly misspelled. The table on page 102 lists twenty-five words that are often misspelled. Be sure you know them perfectly.

A Few Important Spelling Rules

1. Use *i* before *e*, except after *c* or when sounded like *ay*.

   Examples of the rule: ceiling, niece, piece, neighbor
   Exceptions to the rule: foreign, weird, neither, either, their, seize, height

2. When you add the suffix *–ness* to words that end in *n*, keep the *n*.

   Examples: leanness, plainness

3. When you add the suffix *–ly* to words that end in *l*, keep the *l*.

   Examples: carefully, helpfully

4. The *seed* sound in verbs is usually spelled *–cede*. There are only four exceptions.

   Examples: recede, secede, concede, precede
   Exceptions: exceed, proceed, succeed, supersede

5. When you add a suffix that begins with a consonant to a word that ends in a consonant plus silent *e*, keep the *e*.

   Examples: hope + *–ful* = hopeful, face + *–less* = faceless
   Exception: whole + *–ly* = wholly

6. When you add a suffix that begins with *a* or *o* to a word that ends in *–ce* or *–ge*, keep the *e*.

   Examples: courage + *–ous* = courageous
   notice + *–able* = noticeable

7. Add an *–es* to most nouns and verbs that end in *–s*, *–ch*, *–x*, or *–sh*.

   Examples: kisses, catches, foxes, dishes

8. Double the final consonant when adding *–ing* or *–ed* to a word that ends in a single vowel followed by a consonant.

Examples: run + *–ing* = running
get + *–ing* = getting
rub + *–ed* = rubbed
dip + *–ed* = dipped
drop + *–ed* = dropped

Twenty-five Words Commonly Misspelled

1. across
2. all right
3. argument
4. calendar
5. criticize
6. develop
7. doesn't
8. foreign
9. government
10. grammar
11. leisure
12. library
13. necessary
14. possess
15. privilege
16. recognize
17. rhythm
18. separate
19. succeed
20. surprise
21. synonym
22. tragedy
23. truly
24. twelfth
25. unnecessary

SUBJECT

The words in a sentence that tell what or whom the sentence is about are called the *complete subject* of the sentence.

   The barren trees stand in the snow.

The most important word in the subject is called the *simple subject*. The simple subject is always a noun or pronoun. The word *trees* is the simple subject in the example above.

A singular subject must be followed by a singular verb and a plural subject must be followed by a plural verb.

The laughing *child* jumps up and down.

The laughing *children* jump up and down.

Some sentences have two or more subjects. Subjects connected by *and*, *or*, or *nor* are called compound subjects.

compound subj.

Both the *boy* and *girl* take care of the plants.

compound subj.

Neither the *boy* nor the *girl* takes care of the plants.

Notice that a compound subject connected by *and* is always followed by a plural verb. If the compound subject is connected by *or* or *nor*, the verb agrees with the subject closer to the verb.

In English the subject usually comes before the verb. To find out the subject in a sentence that is not in the normal order, ask yourself the question, "Whom or what is the sentence about?" Then change the order in your head.

subj.   subj.

Where is *he* going?   *He* is going where?

subj.   subj.

Here is my *house*.   My *house* is here.

compound subj.   compound subj.

Has *Joe* or *Jack* come home?   *Joe* or *Jack* has come home.

SUBJECT–VERB AGREEMENT

Use a singular subject with a singular verb and a plural subject with a plural verb. Most of the time you can depend on what sounds right to you.

Correct: The *boy is* late today with the paper.
Correct: The *boys are* late today with their papers.

In some cases you cannot depend on what sounds right to you. The chart below lists the most common subject-verb agreement problems. A model sentence is given, showing the correct form. Then the rule is explained. Study the chart carefully to be sure you understand all these problems.

The Rule	The Model Sentence
1. The subject, not the predicate noun, determines the number of the verb.	1. The biggest problem is careless errors.
2. *Doesn't* is the third person singular form.	2. He doesn't look well to me.
3. A modifier coming between the subject and verb does not affect their agreement.	3. The vote of the teachers was unanimous.
4. Amounts of time, money, and distance are singular when one measure is meant.	4. Three years is a long time to wait.
5. Indefinite pronouns like *each* and *body* and *one* words (*everybody*, *someone*) are singular.	5. Each of the girls was invited.

The Rule	The Model Sentence
6. *Either* and *neither* as subjects are singular.	6. Either of these books is all right to read.
7. With a compound subject, the number of the noun closer to the verb determines the number of the verb.	7. Either the coach or the players are in error.

TENSE OF VERBS

English verbs are usually said to have six different tenses. The tense of the verb shows the time of the action. The tenses, their forms, and their uses are listed below.

Tense	Form	Use
Present	Singular usually ends in *–s*	1. To show something happening now: He scores! 2. To tell about something that usually happens: I like vegetables. 3. With an adverb of time, to tell about something that will happen: We leave tomorrow.
Past	Usually ends in *–ed*	To tell about something that happened in the past: I walked home.
Future	*Shall* or *will* with main verb	To tell about something that will happen: I will see you tomorrow.
Present perfect	*Has* or *have* with main verb	To talk about a past action that still continues: We have lost three games so far.

Tense	Form	Use
Past perfect	*Had* with main verb	To tell about a past action that took place before some other past action: I *had seen* him before he saw me.
Future perfect	*Will have* or *shall have* with main verb	To tell about some future action that will take place before some other future action: By the time we get to the corner the bus *will have left*.

The present tense form and the past tense form are the only two forms that can be used in a sentence without helping verbs. As a result, they are sometimes considered the two basic tenses of English verbs.

Do not change the tense of verbs unnecessarily. These examples illustrate this point:

Necessary change in tense:

future
I shall always remember that
past
day when I first learned to ski.

Unnecessary change in tense:

past
He came into the room and
present
then he begins to scold me.

THESIS SENTENCE

The thesis sentence is a sentence that states the main idea of
your essay. A thesis is a belief or conclusion. The thesis
sentence usually comes in the first paragraph of a longer
essay. The thesis sentence is underlined in the paragraph
below.

   The search for cheaper energy has led many people to
install wood stoves in their homes. Wood in many sections
of the country is so plentiful that it is much cheaper than
oil or gas. <u>Wood stoves, however, can be a fire hazard if
they are not installed safely and used correctly.</u>

TOPIC SENTENCE

Paragraphs are about a single idea or topic. The topic sentence
is the sentence that states the main idea or topic of the paragraph. Most paragraphs have topic sentences, but not all
paragraphs do. In the following paragraph, the topic sentence
is underlined:

   <u>This summer seemed very short to me</u>. Before I even got
bored, it was time for school again. I was so excited about
using my new bike, visiting my aunt in Vermont, and
playing in the baseball tournament that time seemed to fly
by. I wish the school year would pass as quickly.

   Notice that all the other sentences in the paragraph explain
or support the main idea expressed in the topic sentence. The
paragraph is not about bike riding or school starting. It is
about how fast the summer went by. All the other sentences
are related to that idea.

Writing a good topic sentence helps you organize what you want to say. Start by deciding on a subject for your paragraph. Think about what interests you. What is your point of view about the subject? Different writers choose the same topic but have quite different topic sentences because they think differently about the subject.

A summer storm is a beautiful, exciting thing to watch.
Summer storms always scare me.

The writer of the first paragraph might describe the flashes of light in the sky. She might explain how she feels during the storm and where she sits for a good view. The second writer might give examples of lightning striking or how to hide during the storm. The two topic sentences would produce two very different paragraphs because the writers have different points of view.

Here are three questions that you can ask yourself to test whether you have a good topic sentence for a paragraph.

1. Does my topic sentence include the subject I want to write about?

2. Does my topic sentence express one idea?

3. Does my topic sentence express a point of view?

Topic sentences are usually at the beginning of the paragraph, but they do not have to be. You may want to put your topic sentence at the end or in the middle of the paragraph.

TRANSITIONS

A transition is a word or phrase that shows how ideas are related. The main types of transitions are shown below, with the most common examples for each.

Transitions that count:	*first, to begin with, second, next, then, finally, in addition*
Transitions that show importance:	*the least important, the most significant, a major factor, a minor consideration*
Transitions that show cause:	*for this reason, therefore, consequently, as a result*
Transitions that connect examples:	*for example, for instance, a case in point, to illustrate*
Transitions that show contrast:	*on the other hand, yet, however, despite this, one difference*
Transitions that suggest comparison	*in the same way, similarly, also, again, in like manner*

TRITE EXPRESSIONS

A trite expression is a phrase or an expression that has been used so much that it seems stale. Trite expressions are sometimes called *clichés*. Avoid the trite expressions listed below, or any others that you recognize as stale.

better late than never

beyond the shadow of a doubt

easier said than done

the facts of life

few and far between

free and easy

a good time was had by all

it goes without saying

the last straw

off the beaten track

a miss is as good as a mile

pride and joy

proud owner

rude awakening

shot in the arm

sink or swim

strike while the iron is hot

truth is stranger than fiction

U   UNDERLINING

Underlining sets apart certain words from the rest of the sentence. Underline the following kinds of titles.

Book title:	I enjoyed <u>The Pearl</u>.
Magazine title:	I like to read <u>Motor Trend</u>.
Movie or play title:	Have you ever seen <u>Mousetrap</u>?
Work of art:	Rembrandt's <u>Nightwatch</u> hangs in a museum in Amsterdam.
Boat or ship name:	I call my boat <u>Sink-or-Swim</u>.

VAGUENESS

Vagueness in writing comes from not being specific enough. The writer uses too many general terms and does not give enough specific information. Vagueness in writing leaves the reader confused and uncertain. Contrast this vague paragraph with the more specific one that follows it.

The weather was bad, and they predicted it would get worse. But they decided we should go anyway. So we started off. We drove for a really long time. I felt awful.

Freezing rain covered the roads, and the forecasters predicted a heavy snowfall. But my parents decided we should begin our trip to our grandparents' farm. So we finally left at 10:30 in the morning, after waiting two hours for the driving conditions to improve. We drove for three hours without stopping. I began to feel nauseated.

Avoid vague adjectives like *bad*, *awful*, *wonderful*, *good*. Avoid the vague noun *thing*. Give as much specific detail as you can.

VERBS

A verb is a word that shows action or a state of being. Verbs are usually classified into four main types.

Type	Definition	Examples
Transitive	An action verb that takes a direct object	I *hit* the ball.
Intransitive	An action verb that does not take an object	The sun *shines* brightly.
Be	Any form of the verb *be* used as a main verb	He *is* my friend.
Linking	A verb (usually of the senses) followed by an adjective or, in the case of the verb *become*, by a noun	The apple *tastes* good. The student *became* a teacher.

Verbs are also said to have two voices, *active* and *passive*. In the active voice, the subject is the doer of the action: I hit the ball. In the passive voice, the subject is the receiver of the action: The ball was hit by me.

In writing description or narration, be sure to use specific verbs that help picture the action vividly.

Vague Verbs	More Specific Verbs
"Come here," he *said*.	"Come here," he *barked*.
I *walked* down the country road.	I *ambled* down the country road.
The dog *ran* from me.	The dog *scurried* from me.

VERB USAGE

Verbs have four main forms.

1. **Present or infinitive:** He *walks*. They *walk*.

2. **Progressive:** He *is walking*. They *are walking*.

3. **Past:** He *walked*. They *walked*.

4. **Perfect:** He *has walked*. They *have walked*.

Regular verbs form the past and the perfect by adding –*d* or –*ed*. Irregular verbs form the past and perfect in special ways. The most important irregular verbs are listed below. Check carefully on the forms about which you are not sure.

Three pairs of verbs cause special problems: *lie*, *lay*; *sit*, *set*; *rise*, *raise*.

1. *Lie* is an intransitive verb. It does not take an object. It means "to be in a reclining position." Here are its main forms used correctly.

Present:	I *lie* down every afternoon.
Past:	He *lay* down yesterday.
Progressive:	She *was lying* here a minute ago.
Perfect:	He *had lain* there for an hour.

Lay is a transitive verb. It takes an object. It means "to put or place." Here are its forms used correctly.

Present:	I always *lay* my books on the table.
Past:	He *laid* the book on the table.
Progressive:	She *was laying* her books in place.
Perfect:	His mother *had laid* them on the table.

2. *Sit* is usually intransitive. It usually does not take an object. It means "to be in a sitting position."

Present:	I *sit* on the porch in summer.
Past:	He *sat* on the chair.
Progressive:	The cat *is sitting* on my chair.
Perfect:	You *have sat* there for three hours.

Set is usually a transitive verb. It usually takes an object.

Present:	The children usually *set* the table.
Past:	He *set* the table.
Progressive:	He *is setting* the table.
Perfect:	She *had set* the table.

3. *Rise* is an intransitive verb. It does not take an object. It means "to move or go up." Here are its forms.

Present:	The sun *rises*.
Past:	The children *rose* early.
Progressive:	Prices *are rising*.
Perfect:	Their voices *had risen*.

Raise is a transitive verb. It takes an object. It means "to grow, lift, or move higher."

Present:	I *raise* the shade every morning.
Past:	He *raised* his hand.
Progressive:	They *are raising* our pay.
Perfect:	My class *has raised* two hundred dollars.

Common Irregular Verbs

Present or Infinitive	Past	Perfect (with *has*, *have*, *had*)
begin	began	begun
blow	blew	blown
break	broke	broken
burst	burst	burst
choose	chose	chosen
come	came	come
do	did	done
draw	drew	drawn
drink	drank	drunk
drive	drove	driven
fly	flew	flown
go	went	gone
grow	grew	grown
know	knew	known
ride	rode	ridden
ring	rang	rung
run	ran	run
see	saw	seen
sing	sang	sung
steal	stole	stolen
swim	swam	swum
swing	swung	swung
write	wrote	written
tear	tore	torn
throw	threw	thrown

W WORD CHOICE

If you are told that your word choice is poor, you probably have made one of the following mistakes:

1. Used slang in formal writing. Use slang only when you wish to suggest a casual tone.

2. Used a colloquial expression in formal writing. A colloquial expression is a phrase like *a lot*, which is acceptable only in conversation or very informal writing.

3. Used a trite word or expression. A trite word is one that is over-used, like *fantastic*, *fabulous*, *wonderful*.

4. Used a vague word instead of a specific one. Avoid vague words like *thing*, *bad*, *good*, *nice*.

5. Used a word with the wrong meaning or denotation. For example, many students confuse *affect* and *effect*. Check pages 120–127 in this handbook for words that are commonly confused.

6. Used a word with an inappropriate connotation. A connotation is the images and feelings associated with a word. If, for example, you wanted to compliment a person, you would call him or her *slim*, not *skinny*.

7. You have repeated a word unnecessarily when you should have used a synonym or a pronoun.

When you have finished writing an essay or a report, check to be sure your word choice is correct.

WORDINESS

Eliminate all unnecessary words in your writing. Try to be as concise as possible. Here are some useful ways to make your writing more concise:

1. Omit empty expressions. Empty expressions are phrases like *if you ask me*, *in my opinion*. They are like "fillers" and they add little meaning to your writing.

2. Eliminate redundant expressions. A redundant expression says the same thing twice, like *old antiques* or *new innovations*. The word *antiques* suggests "old," and *innovations* suggests "new."

3. Use the simplest grammatical structure that expresses your ideas clearly and correctly. Grammatical structures can be arranged from the most simple to the most complex, like this: word . . . phrase . . . clause . . . sentence. The rule of simplicity says, "Use a clause instead of a sentence, a phrase instead of a clause, a word instead of a phrase." Notice how each expression below becomes simpler.

Sentence: The man tried to fix the snowmobile. He had red cheeks and greasy hands.

Clause: The man who had red cheeks and greasy hands tried to fix the snowmobile.

Phrase: The man with the red cheeks and greasy hands tried to fix the snowmobile.

Word: The red-cheeked man with greasy hands tried to fix the snowmobile.

One way to improve your writing is to go over it and strike out every word you really don't need.

A LIST OF WORDS COMMONLY CONFUSED

You will find below several groups of words that are often confused. The words are in alphabetical order. If you are not sure which word to use when you are writing, check this list. Check your dictionary for words not in the list.

a

Use *a* before a word starting with a consonant sound.

His appetite is *a* hopeful sign.

an

Use *an* before a word starting with a vowel sound.

He is *an* honest man.

accept

A verb meaning "receive."

I *accept* your gift with thanks.

except

A preposition meaning "other than."

She invited everyone *except* me.

advice

A noun meaning "help, suggestions."

She gave me good *advice*.

advise

A verb meaning "to give advice."

What did you *advise* her to do?

affect

A verb meaning "to influence."

How did that *affect* you?

effect

A noun meaning "a result."

What *effect* did that have on you?

all together

Everyone together.

Our family is *all together* now.

altogether

Completely.

You are *altogether* wrong.

already

By that time, before now.

We had *already* gone.

all ready

Everyone ready; completely ready.

Are you *all ready* to go?

alright

This is the wrong spelling of *all right*.

all right

This is the correct form. Always use this form.

Is it *all right* for me to be here?

among

Use this word to mean "in the middle of" when you refer to three or more.

There is a good feeling *among* the members.

between

Use this word to mean "the space or time separating things," usually referring to two items.

He divided the apple *between* Tom and me.

amount

Use *amount* to refer to things that can be measured.

He has a large *amount* of candy.

number

Use *number* to refer to things that can be counted.

There was a large *number* of people at the game.

beside

A preposition meaning "next to."

He sat *beside* me.

besides

An adverb meaning "in addition to."

Besides being angry with you, I am also disappointed.

borrow

To take temporarily.

May I *borrow* this rake?

lend

To give temporarily.

Will you *lend* me your rake?

bring

To carry something toward the person speaking.

Bring me that paper.

take

To carry something away from the person speaking.

Will you *take* this to your mother, please?

capital
Location of government.
  Boise is the *capital* of Idaho.
Money for investment.
  Our *capital* has aided other countries.
Very important.
  Murder is a *capital* offense.
A raised letter.
  Use a *capital* with proper nouns.
capitol
The building in which a law-making group meets.
  You can see the dome of the *capitol*.

counsel
Verb: to give advice.
  Did he *counsel* you well?
Noun: advice.
  He gave me good *counsel*.
council
A group of persons who advise.
  I belong to the student *council*.

emigrate
To leave a country; use with *from*.
  Many Jews have *emigrated from* the Soviet Union.
immigrate
To come into a country; use with *to*.
  They *immigrated to* the United States.

farther
Use with distances that can be measured.
>   Walk a bit *farther* with me.

further
Use with matters of degree that cannot be measured.
>   Let us study the matter *further*.

fewer
Use with things that can be counted.
>   I have *fewer* apples.

less
Use with things that cannot be counted.
>   He has *less* ability than she has.

formally
In a formal manner.
>   She was dressed *formally*.

formerly
Previously.
>   I *formerly* attended that school.

in
Within a place.
>   Jayne was sleeping *in* her room.

into
Movement toward an inside place.
>   Jayne went *into* her room.

its
The possessive pronoun.
>   The horse hurt *its* foot.

it's
The contraction meaning "it is."
>   *It's* a fine day.

kind, sort

Both these words are singular.

I like that *kind*.

Do not use *a* after *kind of* or *sort of*.

This *kind of* tree is subject to disease.

Do not use *kind of* or *sort of* to mean *rather*.

I am *rather* tired.

learn

To acquire knowledge.

It's easy to *learn* how to spell.

teach

To help someone acquire knowledge.

Teach me how to spell.

leave

To go; to let stay.

The train will *leave* soon.

Leave the window open.

let

To permit.

Let the dog go.

like

A preposition.

It tastes *like* strawberries.

as

A conjunction.

It tastes *as* it should.

loose
Not attached.
> The boat is *loose*.

lose
To misplace.
> Did you *lose* your money?

principal
Main.
> The *principal* factor is our morale.

The head of a school.
> The *principal* is ill today.

principle
Rule or code of conduct.
> It was a *principle* of his never to gamble.

respectfully
With respect.
> He signed the letter "respectfully yours."

respectively
In the order listed.
> The first three prizes went to Tom, Sue, and Mary, *respectively*.

stationary
Not moving.
> That sign is *stationary*.

stationery
Writing paper.
> Use the best *stationery* you have.

their
The possessive pronoun.
  They brought *their* books.
there
The adverb meaning "in that place."
  Put it *there*.
they're
The contraction meaning "they are."
  They're good people.

too
Also, excessive.
  You *too* are invited.
to
In that direction.
  He gave it *to* me.
two
The number.
  Two of us are eligible.

who's
The contraction.
  Who's your friend?
whose
The possessive.
  Whose book is this?

your
The possessive.
  She is *your* friend.
you're
The contraction meaning "you are."
  You're wrong about that.

INDEX

Encyclopedia article
  bibliography form for, 16
  footnote for, 51
End punctuation, 45
Envelope
  address on, 3
  addressing, correct form, 46
  for business letter, 21
-es, adding, 101
Essay
  concluding paragraph for, 34
  of opinion,
  organization in, 68-69
  persuasive, 76-77
  thesis sentence, 108
  See also composition
Example, 73
Examples, transitions connecting, 110
Except, accept, 120
Exclamation mark, 45, 46, 97
Exclamatory sentences, 97
Exposition
  definition, 47
  kinds of, 47
  writing, 47-48

Family relationships, capitalizing, 23
Farther, further, 124
Fewer, less, 124
Fiction, 64
Figures of speech, 81-82
  definition, 49
Following, colon after, 25
Footnotes, 91
  correct forms for, 50-51
  when to use, 50
  where to put, 50, 51
Formally, formerly, 124
Fragments, 51-52, 94
Friendly letter
  closing, 52, 53
  commas in, 52, 53
  form for, 53

  salutation, 52, 53
  salutation, comma after, 26
Further, farther, 124
Future perfect tense, 107
Future tense, 106

General adjectives, 5
Geographical names, capitalizing, 22
God, gods, 23
Good, using correctly, 63
Grammatical structures, simple, 119

Heading
  of business letter, 19
  of friendly letter, 53
Headings
  of outline, 70-71
Hyperbole, 49
Hyphen, 54

I, capitalizing, 22
i before *e* except after *c,* 100
Images, sensory 93-94
Immature writing, 24
Immigrate, emigrate, 123
Imperative sentences, 97
Importance, transitions showing, 110
In, into, 124
Indefinite article, 13
Indefinite pronouns, 84
  singular, 104
Indenting, 55-56, 72
Independent clauses, 24, 31
Indirect object, 67
Indirect question, 45
Infinitive, 115-117
Infinitive phrase, 78
-ing, adding, 102
Inside address of business letter, 19
Interrogative sentences, 96
Interview, bibliography form for, 16
Into, in, 124
Intransitive verbs, 114, 115